The Smart
Elementary School Teacher

Essential Classroom Management, Behavior,
Discipline and Teaching Tips for Educators

Contents

Chapter 1: Introduction 5

  Roles of an Elementary School Teacher 10

  What is Classroom Management? 12

  Who Benefits from Classroom Management? 14

  How This Book Will Help You 17

Chapter 2: Setting Up Rules and Expectations 20

  Setting up the Rules 25

  Setting Classroom Expectations 31

Chapter 3: Classroom Organization for Success 33

  Seats 34

  Making the Most of Your Classroom Walls 45

  Classroom Organization and Discipline 47

Chapter 4: Classroom Habits for Student Motivation and Focus 48

  How to Start the Class Each Day 49

  Avoid Negatively Labeling Students 52

  Choose Positive Language Over Negative Language 54

  Great Words to Use Everyday 57

Chapter 5: Building a Great Relationship with Your Students 60

  Respect and The Law of Reciprocity 66

  Being a Role Model 69

Chapter 6: Engaging Different Types of Learners in the Classroom 73

  Delivering a Well-Rounded Lesson 77

Chapter 7: How to Encourage Interactive Learning 83

Chapter 8: How to Make Teaching Fun for Everyone 95

Chapter 9: How to Add Movement into The Classroom for Greater Student Focus 105

Creative Ways of Adding Movement In Your Class 107

The Benefits of Adding Movement in the Classroom 115

Chapter 10: How Personalized Learning Opportunities Can Boost Motivation 119

What is Personalized Learning? 121

Benefits of a Personalized Education Program 123

Strategies to Implement Personalized Learning in Your Class 127

Chapter 11: Celebrating the Success of Your Students in Class 134

10 Ways That You Can Celebrate Student Success in Class 136

The Benefits of Celebrating Your Students' Success 145

Chapter 12: Parent Connection Strategies to Build Powerful Relationships 146

Chapter 13: Common Teaching Mistakes to Avoid 157

Chapter 14: Maintaining Discipline and Helping Challenging Students 172

Setting Up the Rules 173

Keeping Track of Discipline 178

Do's and Don'ts of Disciplining 181

Enhancing Communication and Collaboration 183

How To Minimize Discipline Issues 184

Helping Challenging Students 188

Conclusion 192

Teaching should be such that what is offered is perceived as a valuable gift and not as a hard duty.

— Albert Einstein

Chapter 1: Introduction

One of the greatest revolutionaries of our time, Nelson Mandela, once said, "Education is the most powerful weapon you can use to change the world."

Education is about changing the world and making it a better place for us, for future generations, and all the species on the planet. On a more individual level, the purpose of education is the integral development of a young boy or girl, so that they can lead a happy and fulfilled life.

Education enables eager minds to become critical thinkers, to live their lives to their fullest potential and helps them contribute positively to society.

All of that depends upon schooling. More specifically, it begins with the classroom - and with you! As their elementary school teacher, one of your primary roles is classroom management. Good classroom management strategies on the part of the teacher helps students learn well, grow into a better version of themselves, connect and build relationships with their teacher. It makes the classroom environment a nurturing and wholesome place where learning and fun are given preference over everything else.

Classroom management, as you'll discover throughout this book, will make your day-to-day life much easier and will enable your students to focus and become more successful in class.

While education at any level significantly impacts students, one of the most critical periods for a student to learn new things and grasp new concepts is the age of 5 to 10 - in elementary school. Children between those ages can take advantage of their rapidly developing brains, which makes it a powerful time to teach them the fundamental lessons that will stay with them for their lives. From basic arithmetic to learning how to form and write sentences, every lesson taught at that age is critical for their future.

Your primary role as a school teacher is educating those young minds and interacting with them daily within your classroom. Whether you teach them English or Science, everything you teach them will stay with them for the rest of their lives and lay the foundation for future academic endeavors.

Future doctors, scientists, lawyers, authors, artists, mathematicians, and world leaders are within that classroom.

Now it might be a little tricky to imagine the next president sitting in your class while they still play with LEGOs and eat raw cookie dough straight out of the bowl - but that's exactly what's at stake here: the future of the next generation.

As an elementary teacher, your responsibilities extend beyond just delivering lessons to the classroom. As with parenthood, the younger the child, the more responsibilities fall upon you as their teacher and role model.

This book will share with you the proven tips & strategies to help you confidently manage your class, delight your elementary students, de-stress, set clear boundaries for great discipline and behavior in your classroom, feel in control and love your job.

So let's get started!

Roles of an Elementary School Teacher

"If you can read this, thank a teacher" *Bumper sticker, USA.*

As their teacher, the classroom is your domain where you must create a positive environment that encourages students to learn as much as possible. This includes recognizing different students' abilities and creating a lesson plan that uniformly educates every child to maximize lesson retention.

The elementary school teacher is also responsible for ensuring children's social and personal development by providing them with concrete tools and strategies to improve cognitive skills, self-confidence, decision-making skills, and critical thinking. And effective classroom management strategies are a big part of this!

Elementary school children need interpersonal, mental, and physical growth. That's where you, as the teacher, step in. A big challenge for the teacher is developing innovative lessons while adhering to the approved curriculum. Whether by setting up special activities or creating classroom situations where the students utilize their faculties, you have to orchestrate learning opportunities that deliver deep, impactful, and informative lessons.

However, the most significant role that a teacher has to perform is that of classroom management. On one end of the spectrum, novice teachers can be daunted by the notion of managing an entire class by themselves for the first time. But even if you are an experienced teacher, there are still ways we can all learn and improve our skills and strategies to help our students.

Effective classroom management skills are critical to establishing a developmentally appropriate, inclusive, safe, and positive learning environment for the students.

What is Classroom Management?

Are some teachers natural-born Jedis who can harness the power of the Force and use it to their advantage to manage an otherwise chaotic classroom?

Or is classroom management a science that has to be studied over many years until perfected? Is it a form of art you must practice until you get it right? Or can ANYONE learn these skills in a short period of time?

Classroom management is about creating a structured learning environment with rules and regulations that promote learning and developing solutions that reduce or eliminate behavioral issues that might get in the way of learning.

A teacher has to utilize a wide array of skills, tools, and techniques to facilitate the smooth running of their classroom. But it's a skill every elementary school teacher can use, to reduce their stress, feel more in control, engage the students more and love their job!

Of course, managing students should not be confused with being strict and authoritarian. While setting rules and instructing kids to stick to them is an integral part of classroom management, it should never devolve into a rigid regimen that makes the kids resent you rather than look up to you for guidance and inspiration. You and your students are becoming a team together!

Effective classroom management does five things:

· Develops a relationship of mutual respect and appreciation between the student and teacher.

· Trains and reinforces students on how optimal learning takes place within the classroom.

· Makes the best use of time by protecting and leveraging it to increase academic performance.

· Anticipates students' behavior, tackles potential issues within the behavior, and resolves problems that might serve as a hurdle in learning.

· Establishes a standard of behavior that promotes learning, friendliness, and a healthy classroom environment.

Who Benefits from Classroom Management?

Classroom management is not only a great tool for teachers! While it helps us tremendously in the classroom, it directly & indirectly helps others too.

You: As the teacher, classroom management benefits you the most. By using disciplining, teaching, and collaborative techniques, you greatly reduce stress and create an environment where teaching is fun instead of tiring. Successful management will enable you to tap into your energy and passion, letting you focus on what matters: educating the bright, young, curious minds. You will earn the respect of the students, other teachers, the school administration, the parents, and, ultimately, yourself.

The students: The students are there to learn. If the classroom environment does not facilitate learning, it can affect the children for the rest of their lives. However, if the environment is conducive to learning, it will not only strengthen your relationship with them but also create a lifelong desire to learn by setting a rewarding foundation that celebrates their learning process rather than admonishes it. The discipline they learn in the classroom will stay with them for the rest of their lives and shape how they interact with the world. When they learn together in a positive environment, the students will form strong bonds that they'll appreciate and remember for the rest of their lives.

The parents: It is no exaggeration to say that the teacher serves as the third parent to most of their elementary school students, given how much time they spend with them. From dealing with the kids' day-to-day problems to taking care of them, the teacher is a positive role model for their students. Whatever the student takes away from their lessons and the time they spend with you, they reflect on it at home. Successful classroom management benefits the parents of the children by making the child more responsive, intelligent, and empathetic.

The school: Teaching is a collaborative process that relies upon the teamwork of teachers. A lesson the kids learn in mathematics may further their interest in science or technology. Similarly, things they learned in art class will affect how they comprehend creative lessons in English later on. When one teacher successfully manages a classroom, it creates a learning pattern that carries over to other classes in the future, benefiting other teachers in later grades. The techniques have a long-lasting effect that stays with the students when they are promoted to higher grades. Their accomplishments ultimately reflect upon the school. Good classroom management makes sure that the reflection is a positive one.

Society: While it is easy to lose sight of the bigger picture when you have to teach and manage daily, you must remember that the impact you bring about is within society itself. Years from now, the very kids who sit in your classroom will be in charge of science, technology, economics, politics, and contributions to the arts. The discipline that they learn from your classroom will shape them into capable people who can better our society and, in doing so, the world.

How This Book Will Help You

I truly understand how daunting the concept of stepping into a classroom and managing it can be for new teachers. Similarly, I also realize that experienced teachers can struggle with classroom situations, stress and even burnout.

It is for this reason I wrote this book. I wrote this with you in mind. Teaching is a collaborative process. This is me collaborating with you so that you can get the most out of teaching and manage the classroom in the best way possible. And I can't wait to get started!

Together, we will go over the following topics in detail:

· Rules and expectations to create a stress-free classroom.

· Creating the perfect seating plan, stopping trouble before it begins, and setting up your teaching day for success.

· Understanding classroom psychology and habits for motivating students and helping them focus.

- Becoming a teacher that your students look up to and adore.

- Using the four Learning Languages to maximize teaching success.

- Methods to encourage interactive learning.

- Making teaching fun for everyone.

- Ways to add movement to the classroom for greater student focus.

- Personalized learning opportunities and their effectiveness in boosting motivation.

- Celebrating the students' success in the class.

- Connecting with the parents to build powerful relationships.

- Common teaching mistakes to avoid.

- Effective disciplining techniques to stop trouble before it begins.

I strongly believe that equipped with this knowledge, you will unlock your true teaching potential and learn to manage a classroom with ease. And any stress or anxiety you have will melt away! With the techniques you will learn in this book, you will become the teacher that students intently listen to, respect, and look up to. Effective classroom management can change not only your students' lives, but your life too.

Chapter 2: Setting Up Rules and Expectations

"The influence of a great teacher can never be erased"

The first stay of the new school year comes with new challenges, opportunities, and, most importantly, new faces. For new teachers, this is the time to get on top of things, as a great first day can lead to a positive start for the entire year. For experienced teachers, it's a chance to reflect on what they did last year in terms of what worked, what didn't, and what achievements they want to accomplish this year with regard to their students.

Before we can set up expectations and lay down the rules, we have to connect with our students and begin to build the relationship.

Of course, things such as building rapport and memorizing the names of each child will take time. And while there are a hundred different ways to start the first school day, keeping things simple is the best possible way forward. You've got the entire school year ahead of you to pull off great educational feats of learning and bonding with students. Today, it's all about that first impression. Today, it's all about reviewing the rules and setting expectations.

Build Hype About Yourself

A new school year requires an adjustment period not just from teachers but from students as well. In their previous class, they had a favorite teacher whose lessons they loved, whose personality they admired, and whose class they felt most comfortable in. This year, it's your opportunity to be that teacher.

Naturally, your students are just as curious about you as you are about them. Some of them might be nervous, while others will be excited. They want to know who you are, what you like and dislike, and most importantly, whether you're the fun kind of teacher or not. They're trying to figure you out.

Indulge them. Build up excitement about yourself. Do they want to know? Well, you want to tell. If you're adept with video editors, you can make a nice, quirky introductory video about yourself and show it to them. Kids love nothing more than a multimedia presentation on the first day.

If introductory videos aren't your thing, consider brochures or flyers with an overview of who you are and some fun facts about you.

Lastly, you can play a question-and-answer game with them. This allows them to ask the questions they truly want to know.

Why is this important? Once they know you and you have opened up to them, the kids will be more receptive and comfortable around you.

Decorate the Classroom

When you think of the ideal classroom, what is the picture that pops into your mind? For me, the picture is vivid, with bright colors celebrating the spirit of learning all over the classroom. Informative posters and charts sticking to walls, the odd cartoon character reference with a speech bubble promoting a fun scientific fact, and a pleasing coherent theme that brings the whole room together.

Your classroom is almost akin to the children's second home. The aura inside the room holds the potential to inspire them and make them feel welcome. If a classroom is well-decorated, the students will pay more attention to visual disciplinary elements such as rules written on a chart or a performance table.

Setting Goals

This includes setting goals for both you and the students. Given the day-to-day minutia of teaching, sometimes the teacher can lose focus of why they started teaching in the first place. The first day is an excellent opportunity to remind yourself of your purpose. Use that purpose to discover the goals that you hope to accomplish by the end of the school year.

Similarly, setting goals for the students serves as the cornerstone of their academic motivation. You can set weekly or monthly goals as well as a general goal for the year. When students are introduced to goals, it gets them in the rhythm of what to expect and what they can accomplish.

Establish Your Presence

Since this is the first time your students will see you, you should present an authentic version of yourself. We're talking about energy. Whether you're calm and introverted in real life or outgoing and vibrant, the classroom energy you establish differs from your everyday energy. You'll be expected to sustain that energy level throughout the school year.

Establish the Rules

The first day of school is the best time to set ground rules. When you set rules early, you serve to create a healthy and collaborative classroom spirit. It also leads to consistency.

You can set down the rules by sharing them verbally or on a chart on the wall. An effective way to help you students understand the rules is by showing them what each rule would look like in different situations.

When establishing the rules on the first day, keep things short and sweet. You don't want to appear too overbearing or dominating on the first day. Involving your students in setting down some rules will make them feel like they're contributing to the classroom environment and their learning. Have a discussion about what rules would be important to them!

Setting up the Rules

Setting up rules is a necessity in classroom management. When students know the rules, they know what your expectations are. They know what you want them to do, what kind of behavior you don't condone, and what consequences follow after failing the rules.

While going over the rules, the two important factors you must remember while explaining to kids are *what* and *why*.

What: To prevent any misunderstanding and ambiguity, you should go over all the rules and explain each one. For example, the rule "keep your hands and feet to yourself" might need further explanation. You can tell them that you do not want students fighting with each other in the class or annoying other students who are learning.

Make sure you don't talk down to them while explaining the rules. Level with them as if they're rational people who can appreciate you explaining the rules to them. Let them know that you expect them to stick to these rules.

Why: Explaining why a specific rule has been set will help the students appreciate it. Tell them why the rule is for their benefit. For example, the "walk in the hallway instead of running" rule might seem silly and overstrict to students, but if you explain that it's set in place so that no one gets hurt in the hallway, it will help them appreciate the reason you set it.

Some rules are more important than others and must be emphasized multiple times. Use the first day to your advantage to highlight their importance. Let's go over some standard rules and discuss why sharing them with the class on their first day will be a positive step toward setting up expectations.

1. Everyone deserves to learn

Make it clear that your classroom is, first and foremost, a place of learning. A classroom comprises of diverse students with different abilities of learning. If a student disrupts the classroom environment, they are depriving every one of the opportunity to learn.

2. Everyone deserves respect

The classroom contains students from different races, religious backgrounds, and nationalities. It's critical, especially at this early stage in their childhoods, to teach them that everyone deserves respect equally. This rule goes beyond just the dynamics between students. Make them understand that respect is a two-way street. Students who respect their teachers will have their teacher's respect in return. This rule is significant as it teaches students accountability to actions, words, tones, and attitudes.

3. Listen when someone else is talking

During lessons and student participation, it can get overwhelming for the students and the teacher if more than one student tries to speak at the same time. Rather than create an atmosphere of learning, this creates a dissonance that's destructive to the spirit of learning.

Let the students know that everyone's input is valid and important and that they should speak one at a time. They should also learn to listen and wait when it's not their turn. Define a system where everyone knows whose turn it is to speak.

4. Try, try again

A growth mindset is a key element in learning. This rule is meant to encourage students who might get distraught if they're not getting the lessons right. Let them know it's okay to struggle with the lesson as long as they don't give up and keep trying. Create a collaborative environment where students help each other understand difficult topics. Reward their collaboration.

5. Keep your eyes on your work

As you might have noticed, all of these rules have to do with good habits and traits in one way or the other. Similarly, this rule highlights the importance of honesty. You should let them know that if they cheat, they are harming themselves not only in the short term but also in the long run. Tell them it's okay to make mistakes as long as they learn from them. It's not okay to be dishonest and cheat on their tests.

6. Raising your hand is important

The students must raise their hands if they wish to leave their seats or talk to you. This rule serves both the students and the teacher. For the students, it's an opportunity to make their issues known without disrupting the class. For the teacher, the raised hand is a visual indicator of which students need attention. It also instills a sense of order and uniformity in the classroom, which is excellent in creating students' routines.

7. Be kind in speech and action

This rule is about empathy. Our thoughts are unfiltered, most of the time. Our speech should not be so. Explain to the students that everyone has feelings and is capable of perceiving what you say. So, make sure what you say is kind and encouraging. Teach them the meaning of empathy and how it ties in with being kind. The students should be made aware that this isn't just a rule for the class but a general guideline for their entire lives.

8. The custodian's job is to keep the school tidy and safe

The custodians and the janitorial staff are supposed to maintain the school, not clean up after the students' mess. Activities like littering, vandalizing, throwing things at each other, spilling paint and colors on the floor, having food fights in the class, and other disruptive actions will affect the health of the classroom and school as well as add to the responsibility of the caretakers. Emphasize this consequence to the students and establish that your classroom, and by extension the school, will not be a place where the students go about littering.

Setting up these rules and sharing them with the class leads to setting expectations.

Setting Classroom Expectations

An integral part of classroom management is setting expectations. These can be both academic expectations and behavioral expectations. Studies have demonstrated that setting high expectations for your students will make them work to meet and exceed them.

Students can gain a sense of safety and security through consistent classroom expectations. They know what is expected of them, which makes them monitor their behavior and take more responsibility for their learning and behavior. Setting up expectations eliminates a lot of stress for the students and teachers.

You have shared your behavioral expectations with the class by sharing the rules and regulations. Now, by sharing your aspirations with the students, you can also set academic expectations for them. Rewarding good behavior and addressing negative behavior will help you and the class remember the rules.

By becoming more personal with the students, such as remembering their names, likes and dislikes, and backgrounds, you can better understand how to help them manage their expectations. Where someone needs help, help them. Where someone excels, reward them. Where someone makes a mistake, correct their behavior without humiliating them.

You have to understand that these expectations go beyond just the classroom. They dictate how students treat each other, behave with other teachers, and act outside the classroom, such as in the hallways, restrooms, playground, and library.

Chapter 3: Classroom Organization for Success

"I'm a teacher, what's your superpower?"

Classroom organization is the way to go if you want to optimize your teaching while managing the students to ensure an optimal learning environment. An organized classroom gives an impressive impression to the school administration and your colleagues. It speaks volumes about your ability to manage and designate classroom space in the best way possible. A well-organized classroom sends a clear message to the students: This room is meant for you, with your needs in mind.

Let's take a look at some important elements of organizing that will come in handy when you're looking to spruce up the place or liven things up for your students.

Seats

There are many options you can avail yourself of in terms of seating, depending upon factors related to your teaching method. Seats are the vantage points from where students look at you, the blackboard, and the multimedia presentations. They also establish where and when they sit and how they interact with each other.

For example, if you plan to do **lecture-style lessons**, you want your classes to be more teacher-centric. For this approach, you would have to set up the seating to face the front of the room. When all the seats are faced towards you and the blackboard, it will create convenience for all the students when they're looking at a screen or board. For the students, it makes things more comfortable as they're going to stare in one direction for a longer period without having to move a lot.

Now, if you want to create a more **learner-centered experience**, you would set up your seating in groups so the students can partake in group activities and interact easily. A group seating plan will make discussions and collaborations occur organically, letting students take the reins of their learning process and be more confident.

It does not have to be an either-or situation. You can most mix things up by switching the seating depending on the kind of lesson you're teaching. You can also opt for **a hybrid-set up** where the chairs are arranged in groups but face the same direction so that the students can collaborate just as easily as they can look at you and the boards.

When it comes to younger students, another innovative approach to seating is **working on the floor**. Getting rid of the seats all together might seem counterintuitive, especially when a classroom is supposed to instill discipline in the kids. However, floor seating is ideal for kids who have difficulty sitting still in seats for a long time. By allowing them flexibility in movement, you can let them focus on the lesson while taking care of their needs. You'll discover that younger students are more satisfied with working on the floor and are generally more productive.

Recently, science has discovered that prolonged sitting is bad for you. Keeping this in mind, integrate **standing up for some time** as part of the classroom routine so that the children can stay fresh and alert without getting bored of sitting for too long. Consider including group activities that require the kids to stand up for some time.

The benefits of a flexible seating plan include greater collaboration between students, more interaction with the class in general, and increased communication between the teacher and students. As a teacher, you want to facilitate teacher-student interaction and encourage peer-teaching. Flexible seating can help you achieve both results on a level that surpasses the results seen in traditional teacher-fronted settings.

It also makes up for more memorable lessons. Kids are bound to retain the lessons they learned in an interactive and innovative setting compared to traditionally delivered lessons.

The benefit extends beyond just the students. As their teacher, flexible seating allows you to develop new teaching strategies. An open environment with flexible seating lets you explore teaching strategies such as experiential learning and cooperative learning.

Experiential learning: The student "learns by doing" in this type of learning. It's a hands-on teaching method with experiments, simulations, visualizations, and re-enactments. Through experiential learning, a student can better connect theories and knowledge learned in the classroom to real-world scenarios.

Cooperative Learning: By structuring classes in the form of groups, cooperative learning lets students work together in a way that each group member's results affect the entire group's success.

Different seating arrangements also help students focus better by providing a feeling of novelty, complementing the stimulation they receive through their interactive and dynamic classroom setting. This increased focus positively affects their behavior, as educational researcher Sheryl Feinstein noticed in her book *From the Brain to the Classroom*. She mentioned that bland and unchanging school environments cause students to be off task more often than in a flexible seating arrangement. Students seek their own stimulation in fixed environments through movement and disruptive behavior.

Types of Seats:

There's a wide array of seat types to choose from depending upon what kind of theme you're trying to create for the classroom. From the funky wobble stools that give your muscles a thorough workout to the sensible standard desk and chair, you have the freedom to establish the seating in your class.

I would recommend taking the input of the students in this matter. You ensure student participation by going over the different types of seats with them and asking them to explore their options. Student participation is essential because they have to attend class daily. If the classroom reflects their collective personalities, they will feel more at home in the class and more comfortable during the lessons. You can involve the students in creating rules for the flexible seating arrangement, such as by creating a poster containing all probable layouts they can refer to and choose from throughout the year. Rules are important when it concerns seating, such as in the case of ball chairs. In this case, you'll have to set the rule that the students should always keep their feet on the floor to prevent excessive bouncing.

If the students have difficulty understanding or following the rule, you can take their feedback and revisit it, so everyone is clear about what's expected.

At the start of the school year, when you're getting in the flow of things, you should take things slow regarding seating arrangements. Rather than experiment with many different styles, pick one and add it to your classroom. Then see how the class responds before you choose another arrangement.

Regarding seats, if you have input into the buying process, I recommend choosing quality over quantity as those seats will be in rigorous use and prone to wear and tear. Depending upon the class, it's also recommended that you stick to plastic items that don't contain fabric. This will make it easier to clean them at the end of class.

Some examples of potential seats include:

1. Wobble Stools

Besides the obvious wobble effect, the fun part about wobble stools is that they come in a complete spectrum of colors. They're a fun way to add a dash of color to your classroom. The base of the stool is rounded and mobile, allowing you to wobble back and forth. It's very similar to sitting on an exercise ball. They're an excellent way to promote active sitting and engage students' bodies during lessons. However, ensure that you establish a rule against excessive wobbling, as that can cause some students to fall off and injure themselves.

2. Standing Desks

Standing desks are the perfect antidote to sedentary seating. They improve posture, help with circulation, and facilitate burning calories. Standing desks boost one's mood and focus and help them tackle tasks with much more creativity. They come with an adjustable height feature so you can adjust it for students with different heights.

3. Scoop Rockers

Scoop rockers are the latest word in alternative seating. They are cheap and have a low profile that's geared towards comfort. At the end of each lesson, you can scoop them up and stack them in a pile. Their mobility allows for more potential flexible seating arrangements. Like wobble stools, the scoop rockers also come in a wide variety of bright and fun colors.

4. Ball Chairs

Besides their aesthetic appeal, ball chairs are an excellent way for students to work their core muscles while seated. They help increase circulation, improve posture, and decrease discomfort. Students who have difficulty sitting still stand to benefit from ball chairs the most as they can move about on their chairs.

5. Standard Table and Chairs

The good old standard table and chair have been a staple of classrooms for over a century, and for good reason. They are reliable, familiar, and sturdy. Most standard tables have space under the desks where the students can place their belongings. Besides concealed compartments, the standard table and chair sets offer the student enough space in front of them to arrange their notebooks and stationery items while attending the lecture.

Seating Arrangements:

Seating arrangements largely depend on the teaching style you intend to implement. However, the benefit of seating arrangements is that they're very dynamic. You can opt to switch things up every week or every month to keep things fresh. Luckily, there are many different kinds of seating arrangements that you can benefit from:

1. Desks arranged in pairs

If your focus is on group-based exercises, arranging desks in pairs can facilitate students working together. Furthermore, pairing students together will help you sort them easier when delivering papers or answering their questions.

2. Grid

Much like an exam hall, the grid layout has an arrangement where each table or chair is placed equidistant from the other. This layout is ideal for when you want to conduct tests or when you want to encourage children to work alone. However, the drawback with this arrangement is that it greatly limits opportunities like communication between students and group collaboration.

3. Presentation style

By arranging the rows of tables side by side in an arc, you can create a setting tailored for delivering presentations while ensuring that everyone can hear you well. This layout will serve your purpose best if your class includes many student presentations.

4. Groups of four

At the beginning of the school year, you should encourage students to interact with each other and make friends. Arranging the seats in groups of four will allow you to do that. Moreover, this arrangement benefits both individual and small group work.

5. U-Shape

Arrange the seats in a long U shape with the open end of the U facing you. You can monitor the kids easily while encouraging classroom discussion as most children will be sitting face to face with each other.

6. Double-U-Shape

Although the double-U arrangement saves a lot of space, keeping an eye on individual students can get tricky. While it will be harder for larger group activities, the double-U shape does present an advantage for smaller group exercises.

7. Rows

When you have to manage space, arrange the seats in rows. It will be harder to give students individual feedback or review their work in this arrangement. However, it will be much easier for the students to listen to you at the top of the room.

Keep mixing things up once in a while to maintain freshness in the classroom. You can also experiment by mixing up different arrangements to see which works best. You can also change the arrangements depending upon what kind of activity or lessons you have in store for the students. Ask the students for their feedback and see what they like most.

Making the Most of Your Classroom Walls

Besides the classroom seating arrangement, the walls are the most prominent element of the room that you have creative control over. You are encouraged to utilize your artistic skills and creative capacity to make the walls lively with teaching aids, posters, decorations, and demonstrative charts with activities.

From showcasing your students' nonacademic talents and skills to setting up reminders of the rules, there are dozens of possibilities that you can explore when decorating the walls.

· **Content Anchors**

Content anchors are charts that display academic key concepts, important notes, and vocabulary. In a science class, content anchors can have the periodic table on them, chemical compositions of different substances, or an array of different species of plants and animals. In an English classroom, you can have a chart containing various forms of adjectives, verbs, pronouns, and linguistic rules.

- **Rules and Regulations**

Although you have gone over the rules with your students on the first day of class, it's recommended that there be a visual reminder of the golden rules somewhere accessible, and what's more accessible than a wall of your classroom?

- **Academic Hall of Fame**

To celebrate your students' academic success, you can make a chart that showcases exceptional student work. You will have to constantly update the chart to ensure that all the students have an equal opportunity to be recognized for their hard work.

- **Extracurriculars Showcase**

This showcase can celebrate the non-academic achievements of your students, such as works of art, poems, decorations, and even photography. With so many children in your class, there will undoubtedly be many students who have latent talents that you can bring out by showcasing and rewarding them.

Classroom Organization and Discipline

Disciplining students is an essential aspect of classroom organization, especially the seating arrangements.

One example of discipline within classroom management is when students make noise or disturb others during a class. What will you do then? A very non-confrontational manner of resolving issues with troublemakers in class is to split them up.

You can utilize the seating arrangements to your advantage and place the troublesome student with someone more academically inclined and vice versa.

Chapter 4: Classroom Habits for Student Motivation and Focus

"My favorite teacher was my 4th-grade teacher, Miss Binder. Somehow, she brought this shy little girl out of her shell with extraordinary interest and encouragement. She instilled a love of nature, and history, reinforced my love of reading, and most of all, taught me the value of dreams. There's hardly a day that goes by that I don't still feel her influence over 60 years later." — Bev, student.

As their teacher, you are in charge of setting the tone of the class every day. Every little action of yours contributes to the general aura of the classroom. Our students are often very receptive and bright, picking up on the tiniest verbal and nonverbal cues. They can sense if things are off. If the students feel the teacher is ineffective, it may cause them to feel uncomfortable in the classroom and negatively impact their attention and motivation during the lessons.

How to Start the Class Each Day

You can set a positive tone at the start of each class so that the students understand that they're in good, capable hands and can feel comfortable in the classroom. Many little actions contribute to keeping things calm and soothed in the classroom. For instance, greet the students warmly as they enter your class. Compliment them and engage in a few minutes of light, nonacademic conversation before you start the lesson. Think of it as a warmup.

Simple questions such as "how was your weekend?" and "any fun activities you took part in?" can help break the ice at the start of each class. It also humanizes you in the eyes of the students and makes them relate to you better.

Once the class has settled, you should begin with a simple instruction that focuses their attention on the lesson. For example:

"All right, class, settle down, please."

"May I have your attention, everyone?"

Statements such as these focus the class's attention on you. If you want to teach them something from their textbook, you should say, "Please open your book to pages x, y, or z." You can then follow up with the next set of instructions.

If you're delivering a lesson on the board, direct their attention to it by saying, "Now, everyone, please take a look at the diagram on the board."

Once you notice that the class has followed your first instruction, you can tell them what you have in store for them, such as, "In today's class, we're going to learn about the different states of matter." Doing this lets the students know what to expect from today's lecture.

Throughout the class, notice who is being the most attentive and who is having difficulties with the lesson. As their teacher, your job is to ensure that everyone comprehends the lesson and retains the information. So, you should prepare your lesson with everyone in mind.

Take frequent breaks during your lecture to see if the students are following you. Every ten minutes or so, stop the lesson and do a little recap with the students. Maintain an element of interactivity by asking questions from everyone. This keeps the students on their toes and also lets you know whether they understand the lesson or not.

During the lesson, encourage them to ask questions in a positive manner. Let them know that there's no such thing as a stupid question. Validate their queries by listening to them and addressing their issue until you're sure they've understood the concept.

If you're concerned about potential disruptions in the class or if the students will lose track of the lesson, the perfect antidote is creating an intriguing lesson that maintains their interest while delivering the fundamentals of the lesson.

Intertextuality is a technique where you use different pop-culture references concerning the subject matter. It can serve as a very effective tool for teaching. Let's say during science class, you're teaching them about engines. It will add fun to the lesson if you casually mention that Iron Man has propulsion engines in his armor that allows him to fly. Combining the lesson with things the students love, such as comic book characters, video games, or TV shows, will help them connect with you and understand the lesson better. It will also make sure they never get bored.

Avoid Negatively Labeling Students

From a psychological standpoint, negative labeling of students severely limits their learning capability and growth. It chips away at their confidence and hurts their feelings. Using negative labeling in front of the class will lead to the rest of the class mocking the student when you're not there.

Negative labeling is destructive to the spirit of learning. It creates a rift between the student and teacher. The student sees the teacher as an antagonist instead of a friend and confidante. It also creates future problems by potentially turning the student obstinate and rebellious.

Words such as naughty, bad, bold, mischievous, troublesome, stupid, and slow harm the student. If a teacher uses these words with the student, it detaches the student from their educational journey. Instead of seeing it as an opportunity to learn and prosper, they see it as a punishment and humiliation they have to face daily. In the long term, they can evolve into psychological problems that lead to dysfunctional lives.

The derogatory nature of these words perpetuates psychological harm that translates into other facets of the student's life. They'll become jealous of students doing well in class and might bully them. They'll become violent towards their siblings at home. Worst of all, they will have low self-esteem and confidence, which can hinder all their future endeavors, not just learning.

Rather than use negative labels, come up with constructive advice and criticism that they can understand and implement during their time in the classroom. Rephrase that criticism into a set of instructions without admonishing the student.

For example, let's say a student is being very loud and disruptive in class. Instead of scolding them for being naughty and noisy, you can engage them in an activity that makes them a useful part of the class while detaching them from their disruptive behavior. Have them read from their book in front of the class or participate in a student-teacher experiment demonstration. If they feel like they're contributing to the class, they will become more attentive and pay heed to the lesson.

Choose Positive Language Over Negative Language

Building upon the takeaway from the last section, you should not use negative language in class. This includes phrases that begin with "don't". As with negative labels, negative language can greatly limit students' potential, make them feel self-doubt, and hinder the learning process.

Suppose there's a test tomorrow and you want to emphasize that everyone should come prepared.

Rather than say, "For the test tomorrow, don't forget your pencils, erasers, and calculator," you should say, "There's a test tomorrow. I expect you all to be fully prepared. Please bring your pencils, erasers, and calculator."

With just a few changes, you have changed the entire tone of the sentence from a foreboding tone to an advisory tone.

If a student enters the classroom and opens the door, instead of telling them, "Don't slam the door," instruct them positively by saying, "please shut the door quietly." By doing that, you've changed the context of the instruction from a prohibiting one to an assisting one.

When you encounter someone talking in class, your knee-jerk reaction will be to tell them, "Don't talk in class." This might come across as you scolding them. Instead, you can opt for, "Please pay attention to your teacher and peers." Now it's not a scolding anymore as much as it is a gentle request.

Similarly, replacing the phrase "Stop doing this or that" with "Please refrain from this and that" will also change the tone from confrontational to passive.

Why is this important, you might wonder? A classroom is, before anything, a place of learning. A place of learning should foster an environment that encourages, educates, and promotes growth.

Negative language opposes all three elements.

Rather than encourage, it discourages the student from participating in the class. Sometimes they might not even know that they're doing something wrong, and if they get admonished in that instance, they'll feel shocked, even hurt. Instead of educating, negative language serves to deprive. It prohibits further participation in the class, detaching the student from the lesson. Lastly, instead of promoting growth, it forces the student to sink away and focus on the social repercussions of the negative language rather than the lesson.

The teacher is a role model to the students. When students notice a teacher using negative language, they will also enact it in their lives. But if a teacher uses positive, encouraging language, it will make the students friendly and mild-mannered. It will also make the students respect the teacher more, creating a great relationship between you and them.

Great Words to Use Everyday

When you think back to your favorite teacher and class in school, what sticks out? Do you remember the teacher being encouraging? Do you remember that they were friendly and patient? What did they do to make you enjoy the class?

As you will have noticed, there are different kinds of students in the class. Some are energetic and overzealous, whereas others are introverted and shy. You want all of them to participate freely within the class. An encouraging tone between students and their teacher helps set a positive, calm, and motivating environment for everyone.

Encouraging words and phrases is the best way to ensure everyone feels welcome in the class, especially the introverts. However, the phrases shouldn't be overly sweet, otherwise, they can convey a sense of false praise and condescension.

When you notice a student excelling at a lesson, praise them with a "Great job!" or "A for Effort!"

If you notice that certain students are struggling to understand the class's concepts, you may foster a growth attitude in them by telling them things like, "I can see you're really trying hard, and I appreciate it," or "It's not your fault, this lesson is challenging, but together we can get through this". For students prone to anxiety, encouraging phrases such as these will help calm them down and trust you. This lets them know you're on their side instead of an opponent.

Some examples of great phrases you can use to inspire and validate students include:

"You've got this!"

"Excellent work!"

"I like the way you think."

"Your solution was very creative."

"I knew you could do it."

"Congratulations!"

"I'm proud of you."

"Wow. You must have been practicing at home."

"I love hearing your ideas."

"What an awesome improvement."

"You kept trying and finally did it."

"I commend you for your teamwork."

"I have complete confidence in your abilities."

You'll make your students self-reliant, confident, and independent through these encouraging phrases and words of wisdom. You'll boost their problem-solving capabilities and allow them to try without fear of failure.

The best part about using encouraging terms is the sheer joy on your student's faces when they get praise from you. Your encouragement will prove that they get rewarded for making an effort, setting the foundation for future success.

When the students know that their teacher appreciates them, they go the extra mile to impress you, work hard, and maintain your expectations from them.

Chapter 5: Building a Great Relationship with Your Students

"Elementary school teacher: Just like a normal teacher but way cooler"

Effective classroom management is about ensuring the students follow the rules. It's about building a fulfilling relationship with them that help them achieve their goals, solve classroom management issues, and create a wholesome classroom environment. According to the American Psychological Association, building a solid relationship with your students can help them develop socially and academically.

Learning thrives through engaging lessons in a classroom where the teachers and students share a great relationship. The best teacher can maximize the learning potential of each student in their class by unlocking their potential through developing positive and respectful relationships with them.

Building a trusting relationship takes time and can be challenging, especially for new teachers. In time, you can master the art of gaining their trust through mutual respect.

Some strategies that accelerate the development of trust between students and their teachers include:

Making Learning Fun

If you want kids to look forward to your class every day, you need to make learning fun and exciting. Students thrive when they are presented with hands-on, kinesthetic learning activities where they can learn by performing. When you incorporate creative uses of technology in the class, the lesson becomes even more exciting for them.

Engage the students. Make them active participants in the lesson. In a lesson about enzymes, designate the role of active sites, catalysts, and enzymes to the students and let them role-play. Designate chemical identities for the children and have them react with each other to form new chemicals in a lesson about chemical reactions.

Add Humor to the Mix

Teaching should not be boring. Neither should be learning. Students, like most people, enjoy laughter. A little joke goes a long way in breaking the humdrum of boredom in the class. It doesn't have to be a whole comedy routine. No one's expecting you to become a standup comic in the class. Just incorporate simple humor within the class so that no one feels bored. You'll notice that your students respond positively when you make lighthearted humor in class. This will incentivize them to come to your class eagerly, as they'll enjoy the jokes and humor integrated into the lessons.

Offer Structure

Human beings are creatures of habit. We desire order and structure for a sense of stability and security. Your students also want a structure within the classroom that lets them make sense of what will happen and what to anticipate every day.

If a teacher lacks structure, they lose valuable instructional time every day and come across as inexperienced. The students will not respect someone they think isn't capable of teaching them properly. However, if you come prepared from the very first day of school, set down a structure for the classroom time, and ensure that every day that structure is adhered to, the kids will respect you and deeply appreciate the order in class.

Another benefit of providing structure is minimal downtime. With the help of structure, every day becomes loaded with engaging learning activities with barely any downtime.

Teach with Genuine Passion

Excitement is very contagious, as is passion. When you teach with excitement and passion, you draw out the curiosity and passion of your students. If you are enthusiastic about the subject, so will your students. When a teacher shows excitement about a topic, the children become intrigued and become more receptive.

They'll see that you have a passion for the subject. They'll want to impress you with their learning, and you will be leading the students by example.

Use Their Interests to Your Advantage

Just as the students become intrigued by your passion and excitement for the topic, you should also keep an eye out for what the students are interested in. Every student has a passion for something. From robotics to video games, there are numerous topics that kids are excited about. Some envision a future in space, while others want to dive to the depths of the sea and study sea life.

You can find out about their interests using a questionnaire or survey. Once you know their interests, you will have many opportunities to incorporate them into your lessons.

Teachers who go the extra mile and take the time to include their students' interests will notice increased participation, higher involvement, and better learning in general.

Not only will your students appreciate you taking an interest in them, but they'll also want to do right by you by exceeding your expectations.

Stay Positive, Especially When It's Tough

Sometimes, you'll have a terrible day. It's inevitable. Everyone has awful days, including teachers. Your trials can get difficult to deal with. However, as a teacher, you are responsible not only for your life but for your students' life. Regardless of what's going on with your personal life, you should never let that interfere with your teaching ability.

Positivity is just as contagious as passion and excitement. When your students notice your positivity, they'll be drawn to you like a magnet. You'll inspire them. They'll look up to you as a role model rather than look at you as just a teacher. They'll want to impress you, learn from you, and become your friend.

Respect and The Law of Reciprocity

Earning your students' respect is a huge step in forming a great relationship. According to the Law of Reciprocity, when people receive something, they're compelled to return the favor. Translate that to respect: If you respect your students, they'll be forced to respect you back.

What does respecting your students entail?

First of all, you should never use sarcasm, yell at them, single out a student to punish or humiliate them in front of the entire class, or embarrass them in front of their peers. Doing any of the above will not only make the individual student lose respect for you but also lower your image in the eyes of the entire class.

On the other hand, if you're supportive, encouraging, wise, and friendly, the students will naturally form a bond with you where they'll want to impress you, talk to you, and be like you. That is respect.

In your class, you should handle things professionally when potential issues arise. Talk to them in a respectful manner that's direct and authoritative. If there's a problem, deal with it individually rather than scold the child in front of the entire class.

When dealing with a class, you should treat every student the same. Playing favorites will make the rest of the class lose respect for you as they'll constantly feel that you are biased in favor of one of them over the others.

The same set of rules should apply to all the students. When dealing with students, such as grading their papers or looking at their assignments, you must be fair and consistent with them.

When you're not teaching, be a little frank with them. Ask them about their interests outside of school. Listen to them as they share tidbits from their life with you. Get some one-on-one time with every student throughout the week. One-on-one time is essential for their growth as most students feel their voices aren't heard in a large classroom. During an individualized session, they'll feel like they have your full attention.

Share your stories with them if they're inclined to listen. Storytelling remains one of the easiest ways to connect with your students. Sharing stories from your life, such as the difficulties you faced as a student or how you were once a former student at the same school, will fascinate your students and make them feel like you're one of them.

Don't just clock in at the end of every school day. There are always some student events in the school after hours or on the weekends, such as basketball games, science fairs, talent shows, drama productions, and debates. Go to these events. Be there for your students. Reward them for a job well done in these events. Praise their efforts. Make them feel like you're invested in their efforts beyond just the classroom.

Little by little, the students will start respecting you, all thanks to the Law of Reciprocity.

Being a Role Model

How can you cultivate habits in your students without explicitly telling them to do something? You would like them to speak politely, not use gadgets such as phones and tablets during class, be patient with each other, handle disagreements respectfully, not shout, and listen intently to you.

How can you achieve that? It's simple, by being their role model. Students in the age range of five years to ten years are very impressionable in terms of their habits and behaviors. They look up to their elders to mirror their behaviors. Whereas a bad role model will teach them mischief and disruption, a good role model will cultivate the best habits in them.

Speak Politely with Others

Your students will notice how you speak to them and other people, such as the school staff. Whether they do it consciously or not, subconsciously, they understand your traits and will mimic them. If they notice that you always speak politely and calmly with everyone, this habit will embed in their minds.

Now, when they talk to you, they'll be respectful, and when they go home, they'll mirror your politeness with their family.

Keep Electronics Out of Sight

This is yet another example of do-as-I-do. Using your phone during a lecture in class will make a very bad impression on the students, making them think you're not serious about the lecture. They'll then treat the class with a casual attitude, often turning to their phones and tablets for distraction. If you don't want them to use electronic devices in class, you shouldn't use yours.

So, while teaching them, keep your electronics out of sight and request that they do the same. They'll be inclined to follow your lead if they see that you're also not accessing your electronics.

Handle Conflict Calmly

Eventually, some students will have conflicts with each other. You should play the role of mediator and quickly defuse the situation calmly and rationally. You should bring it to the students' notice that they're equals and deserve each other's respect. Ask them to shake hands, make friends, and refrain from scolding them.

You've just displayed calmness during a conflict in front of the entire class. Believe it or not, this is ingrained in their minds and will soon become a part of their personality.

Never Shout

If you don't want the students to shout and insult each other, you should refrain from shouting in class. Whether during a lecture or to discipline someone who's creating a commotion, shouting is a very disruptive activity that will scare the kids for the time being, sure, but will ultimately make them lose respect for you and become rebellious.

Be Friendly and Approachable

You want to be the teacher whom students can approach easily with any problem they're having, whether it's academic trouble or something personal. Be approachable and friendly so the students can confide in you if something's wrong. You should be someone they feel at home with, someone they're sure will protect them if things go wrong. By being a positive role model to them, you're planting a seed in their subconscious to lend a helping hand wherever they see someone who needs help.

Be Patient

Remember, they're just kids. They're going to make mistakes. They're going to act like kids. They're going to sometimes ignore the rules and be childish. That's because they're children. In those moments, the easier option is to scold or be stern with them for order in the class. Be fair, kind, and patient with them.

Chapter 6: Engaging Different Types of Learners in the Classroom

"My favorite teacher was my 2nd-grade teacher. She was always positive, patient and had fun/interesting activities planned." —Kim, student.

Every student has different learning capabilities. Throughout your teaching career, you'll come across a wide variety of students who respond differently to different types of learning.

You'll notice that some natural visual learners learn best from visual displays of knowledge in the form of charts, graphs, and data. Others will be more auditory-inclined. You'll notice them paying close attention to you while you're lecturing. They'll also be the ones who ask questions and process their learning through speaking and listening. Then there will be students who excel at reading and writing. They'll retain their knowledge by reading books and notes and will take many notes during the class. Lastly, there will be a subset of students who respond to learning by doing. They'll be the ones who enjoy a more hands-on approach to their lessons, such as practical demonstrations.

I've just described the four learning languages, also known as the VARK modalities. The VARK model has four learning techniques, namely:

· Visual

· Auditory

· Reading/Writing

· Kinesthetic

Visual

Students who are visual learners prefer their information in the form of maps, diagrams, charts, flow charts, graphs, and all the symbolic arrows, circles, and hierarchies that you can use within a visual medium. They prefer the correlation of data through visual aids as compared to words. However, visual learning does not include photos, videos, presentations, and animations. You must understand that visual learning is more about the different formats you can use to highlight and convey information in a tabular or graphical form.

Kids who prefer this model of learning will be more inclined towards richer visual data lessons. When you visually show them the relationship between different concepts, they'll grasp it better than other methods. For example, while explaining a scientific process, you can use a flow chart instead of just words to demonstrate how the process takes place.

Auditory

Kids who are more aurally inclined prefer information delivered in the form of speech. They learn best from lectures, group discussions, audio files, webchats, and talking with other students. These students prefer to talk to themselves to reinforce what they have learned. Sometimes, these students will ask questions that they've already asked. They want to hear the answer repeatedly so that the concept clears in their mind.

Kids who prefer this model of learning will thrive in group discussions. You can have the students read the lessons out loud so they can learn as they read to the rest of the class.

Reading/Writing

These are the note-takers, the book-readers. Many teachers and students prefer this mode of learning. Students who prefer this teaching style want to learn through information delivered in the form of words. Text-based input and output such as reading and writing in different formats like manuals, reports, essays, and assignments are the go-to for these students. Students who prefer this learning model strongly prefer PowerPoint presentations, gathering data from the internet, lists, diaries, the thesaurus, and everything that has to do with words.

Engaging kids with this preference for learning is convenient, as most of your lessons will have a reading/writing element.

Kinesthetic

Students who prefer this learning style want demonstrations of what they've learned through experiments, practical scenarios, simulations, videos, and interactive tools that let them get the knowledge in a much more hands-on way. They want to feel the reality and the concrete nature of their lesson. Model toys, starter kits, experiment sets, and graphical simulators are the best way to learn for these kids.

Delivering a Well-Rounded Lesson

As with life, lessons should also be multi-faceted, with different layers working together to deliver a comprehensive lesson. In your class, you should deliver lessons using all four learning modes. Being proficient in one mode of learning does not mean that the student necessarily falls behind in other modes. Those learning modes are preferences. So, you can mix things up in your lesson to cater to different learners to establish that they're all getting the key takeaways from the lesson.

You can do this by creating lessons that include a wide variety of learning methods that allow every student the chance to engage with the material in the best way for them. Let's look at some examples to understand this concept more clearly.

Example: The Water Cycle

A fairly common and fundamental lesson in most elementary school science classes is that of the water cycle, i.e., what happens to water and where it comes from. This includes different stages of water such as condensation, evaporation, the melting of snowcaps, the journey of water from rivers and tributaries to the sea, and so forth. It's a complete cycle showing water's journey and recyclable nature.

Keeping VARK in mind, you can craft a lesson that contains all four modes of learning all the while tackling the subject matter in the following way:

1. Create a visual flowchart or cycle labeling the different stages of water. This will help the visual learners grasp the concept easily. You can use small diagrams as visual aids to highlight rivers, seas, clouds, and so on.

2. Now demonstrate the lesson in written form, complete with bullet points and sentences highlighting each stage of the water cycle. Allow some students to read from the board or their notes so that the rest of the class can listen to them. Deliver a lecture yourself as well to emphasize the significance of the lesson.

3. Give the students a class assignment where they write down their water cycles and devise creative ways to connect different geographical locations with different stages of the water cycle.

4. Conduct a practical study, demonstrating evaporation, condensation, and melting so kinesthetic learners can learn from this exhibition.

By creating a well-rounded lesson around the water cycle, you've included all four learning modes without over-focusing on just one mode. It's a very balanced lesson that uses all the available resources to deliver a learning experience that every kind of learner comprehends.

Example: Gravity

Another common and important topic that kids learn in science, mathematics, and history class is gravity. From a scientific perspective, they learn how gravity affects everything on the planet and how different cosmic bodies have different gravitational fields. From a mathematical point of view, the formula for gravity is often used in different arithmetic problems. From a historical point of view, the journey of how Sir Isaac Newton discovered gravity is an inspiring lesson for every budding scientist in the class.

Regardless of which subject you're teaching gravity as a part of, you can use the VARK model to create a balanced lesson that addresses each mode of learning while ensuring complete comprehension of the subject matter.

1. On the board, create a diagram that showcases how gravity works. The visual representation of gravity should include a chart that demonstrates variables such as force, gravitational constant, the mass of objects, and the distance between their center of masses. You can make it quirky by adding a picture of an apple hitting Isaac Newton's head.

2. Next, describe the lesson as captivatingly as you can using your words. Ensure that the auditory learners pay attention as you explain the visuals you've drawn on the board. Integrate the story of how Isaac Newton discovered gravity and how every modern physics discovery is dependent upon the discoveries of Newton.

3. Write down the formula for gravity and create a few scenarios where such a formula will be useful. Have the class do a few test examples together, alone, or in a group setting.

4. Have some fun with the concept of using science equipment from the lab. Show how a feather and a brick fall to the ground simultaneously thanks to terminal velocity and gravity. Let the class participate in your experiment, so kinesthetic learners can have fun.

Example: Parts of Speech

Even though English is primarily a language class, you can still utilize the VARK model in lessons that teach them about parts of speech. The eight primary parts of speech include nouns, pronouns, verbs, adjectives, adverbs, prepositions, conjunctions, and interjections.

Suppose you're teaching them about verbs and how verbs express actions, occurrences, and states of being.

1. Include a visual demonstration of a person performing an act. Label the person as the subject, the action as the verb, and the object interacting with the verb. A sentence like "Luke kicked the ball" should be highlighted to demonstrate that Luke is the subject, kicked is the verb, and the ball is the object. Create a flowchart that shows how a subject performs different actions and how those actions can be described using verbs.

2. Have half the students in the class perform some designated actions while the other half identify the subject, object, and verb.

3. Make the class write exercises where they identify the verbs, fill in the correct blanks, and create sentences with the verbs they have learned.

4. Invite the students to come to the top of the class and share their sentences. Offer verbal feedback on each sentence and encourage them accordingly.

You've not only demonstrated a visual example with the help of a flow chart, but you've also created a kinaesthetic lesson from a very challenging subject matter. Through the written exercise, you've engaged the reading/writing learners. Also, having the class share their sentences and offer feedback on them gave the auditory learners a solid understanding of the topic.

Chapter 7: How to Encourage Interactive Learning

"Teacher? I prefer the term educational rockstar"

Interactive learning refers to the students participating and engaging with the lesson through various activities and collaborating and interacting with fellow students in the classroom. Interactive learning captures students' attention quickly and efficiently to ensure they're engaged in learning while having fun.

It improves the students' cooperation skills by putting them in situations where they have to collaborate with their peers. This accelerates their growth by allowing them to participate with others, listen to their ideas, and blend them into innovative solutions.

This form of learning is extremely beneficial for the students' critical thinking and problem-solving skills. Interactive learning encourages them to think outside the box and devise different yet valid solutions to the same problem.

Since interactive learning focuses on real-world problems and finding creative solutions to those problems, students have to think critically to come up with solutions to those problems, developing sharper analytical skills. When they grow older, these skills will help them in their careers.

As interactive learning creates a natural opportunity for active learning, students become more engaged with the lesson and genuinely enjoy a thriving process that facilitates accelerated learning.

Let's look at some practical ways to encourage interactive learning.

1. Pairing the Students

As their teacher, you must ensure that the students interact with the lesson and each other to create a spirit of teamwork. If you pair students as reading buddies or lab partners, you create an organic opportunity for them to come together and work together. It will be even more effective if they're paired to perform student-centered activities.

As you may already know, modern teaching has outgrown mere notetaking and lecturing. The advanced teaching methods include activities catering to the students' interests to deliver a more robust lesson. In a lesson about famous American historical figures, pair two students together to create a digital presentation using PowerPoint or Canva.

They can bounce ideas off each other and develop a collective presentation that utilizes both of their skills.

Similarly, if you're engaging them in an English lesson, have two kids collaborate on one summary report of a short story that the class read together. Notice how the students discuss different aspects of the same short story, highlighting facts and features that the others might have missed.

Pairing the students also creates a sense of healthy rivalry within the class as one pair competes with the other.

2. Incorporate Technology

Kids these days take to technology like fish to water. They're naturally adept at using smartphones, tablets, and consoles. If you incorporate technology in your class, you'll engage the part of them that's partial to technology.

From making visual presentations on the computer to online educational games, there are so many potential uses of technology in the class that it baffles the mind. Here, asking the students for their input regarding what kind of technology they want to be incorporated into their lessons would be beneficial.

Some students are eager to learn from video resources such as the ones found on YouTube, Udemy, and Khan Academy. Others prefer online simulations where they can perform digital experiments without the risk of failure.

In a computer science class, you can have them write code on online editors such as Codecademy, where they can watch snippets of code perform miraculous functions.

Innovative learning tools such as touch-screen TVs, the internet of things, and personalized student laptops can create a sense of thrill within the class as they learn their lessons in new and innovative ways.

3. Mockups

Mockups or case studies are real-world simulations of issues that the class has to come together to resolve. Model United

Nations are one form of mockup where kids act as world leaders to resolve global issues.

Within the setting of your classroom, you can introduce the students to a real-world problem such as global warming and then give them a set number of time to come up with different solutions. You can let them use computers and their tablets to consult research regarding their real-world problem.

At the end of the exercise, your students will present different ideas such as using renewable energy sources, reducing the carbon footprint of giant corporations, planting more trees to tackle deforestation, and so on.

This exercise will bring the entire class together as opposed to just a few groups or one-on-one pairing. They will be inclined to participate in this exercise as a whole, taking each other's advice, giving each other useful tips, and presenting their findings as a unified front.

4. Arranging a Day Trip

Let's say you recently covered a lesson on farming as part of your social studies class. It would be an excellent idea to arrange for a day trip on which you take the students to a nearby fully-functioning farm with cattle, crops, and poultry.

You and the farmer can then point out different farm components as you take the kids on a guided tour. The kids can ask questions, interact with different features of the farm, pet the animals, play around a little bit, and have a light picnic at the end.

5. Invite an Expert

Think about it; their primary interaction is with their parents, their friends, and you, their teacher. They don't know many adults who are in different professions. Inviting an adult who's a professional in their respective field intrigues the children and makes them more curious about what kind of world lies in wait for them.

Suppose there's a lesson on space that you recently covered with your class. You discussed the basics of our solar system, the composition of stars, different galaxies, and black holes. This was a theoretical approach.

However, if you invite an astrophysicist from a local university to share some stories with the students, they'll become intrigued by the lesson. Inform the students a day before you invite the expert so they can go home and brush up on what they learned so they can question the expert about all sorts of things.

A lesson about oceans and marine life would be well-complimented by a visit from a marine biologist. A lesson where the class learned about supercomputers would benefit from a visit by, say, game developers who utilize high-level computers to make video games and simulations.

The students can have a question-and-answer session with the expert, the expert can demonstrate some real-world experiments or take them on a tour of their facilities.

6. Group collaborations

Divide the class into small groups and allocate a limited number of resources to each group for them to share. Now, present them with an exercise or problem they must solve. Add a flair of competition to the mix and declare that the first three positions will get some prize.

Move throughout the class as the groups perform their task and notice how they collaborate. Pitch in where you feel like they're struggling with a task.

Tell the class that they'll get additional points for successful collaboration. Similarly, add a few consequences to disruptive behavior. Points will be deducted if the kids misbehave with each other.

These group collaborations don't just have to be for lessons and quizzes. You can sort the class into groups for presentations, experiments, and demonstrations.

Even though it's best to mix things up with different pairings, try and pair the kids with kids they're friends with. Their foundation of friendship will motivate them to work together harder.

7. Think, pair, share

This is a common interactive learning style where the students are presented with a problem, and they must think about to find a solution. After thinking of a solution, they're encouraged to share the solution with their partner before they share it with the rest of the class. After the two discuss their ideas, they can present a unified front and share their concepts with the rest of the class.

Think, pair, share is a very friendly way to enable students to share their thoughts with their peers in a vulnerable and non-intimidating way. When two students guide each other regarding an issue, their confidence in their solution boosts, and they're better able to present their findings to the rest of the class. Likewise, because they had to work hard to develop a collective solution, they will also appreciate other students paired together to present their solutions.

8. Debating

Although this is a fairly traditional form of learning, it is a very viable mode of interactive learning where the students not only interact with each other through lively debate but also depend upon the teacher's feedback.

The way to create a healthy debate in the class is by presenting a statement and picking two sides. One side is in favor of the statement, whereas the other is against the statement. The debates can be individual or group discussions where multiple class members come forward and present their ideas simultaneously.

You, the teacher, will be their judge. You will be responsible for gauging the validity and merits of each point presented by the opposing sides. If a teacher friend of yours is free, you can invite them and have them be the second judge to add more impartiality to the ruling.

This method of interactive learning will get the students to participate in sharing their ideas with the entire class. It will serve as a confidence booster to those who worked hard to come up with legitimate points, and it helps to educate those who were a little behind on their understanding of the lesson.

9. Buzz Session

Like debating, the buzz session involves the entire class by splitting them into two or more groups. You can create groups of students and assign them team numbers or colors. Then you equip each team with a buzzer that they will press every time you ask a question. The team that pushes the buzzer first will answer the question first.

Rather than quiz the class in the traditional way, testing their knowledge retention through a playful and interactive buzz session will get them excited as they compete with each other and wrack their brains to come up with the right answer.

If a quiz isn't your style, you can still use the buzz session to facilitate students in coming together and brainstorming solutions to problems and sharing them with the class.

10. Interactive Notebooks

Encourage your students to take notes creatively by using stickers, highlighters, sticky notes, pencils and pens of different colors, and visual aids such as graphs, tables, and charts.

To spice things up, declare an interactive notebook competition where you'll compare the styles and formats of different students' notebooks and decide which ones are the best.

11. Educational Games

Students of all ages are fond of games. You can make learning more interactive by introducing games into the lesson.

Task cards are an effective style of game that bolsters learning and collaboration between the kids. Place task cards throughout the classroom with different tasks and questions on them. Form groups between the students and challenge them to complete the most tasks within a particular time. You can even up the ante by providing prizes to the groups who perform the best.

In English lessons, you can use Scrabble, Word Hunt, and Crossword to your advantage to teach students new vocabulary.

In lessons concerning classification, you can play the game called Four Corners. In a lesson where the class is learning about mammals, birds, amphibians, and reptiles, designated each corner for each type of animal. Ask the kids to go into the correct corner when you name an animal.

These are some of the ways that you can promote interactive learning in your class. Of course, you are encouraged to come up with creative ideas for interactive learning depending on what kind of students are in your class and their preferences.

Chapter 8: How to Make Teaching Fun for Everyone

"It takes a big heart and a large, extra-strong coffee to shape little minds."

While teaching is primarily about educating the students and ensuring that the topics mentioned in the course syllabus are covered before their exams, the teacher's job entails much more than just teaching. It's the teacher's job to liven things up in the classroom and make everyone feel like they're participating in the lesson. Most importantly, it's the teacher's job to make things fun.

Keeping things fun will not only ensure that the students in your class are happy, but it will also serve as the basis for connecting with them. If you have a strong bond with your students, you will discover that the lessons become almost intuitive. You'll already know the students' first names and what they like, dislike, and excel at. You'll know them at a deeply personal level that will let you resonate with them as you deliver your lessons.

While for some teachers, the process of making things fun seems natural, some of us have to work towards that goal. While previous chapters revolved around how lessons related to children, this chapter is about how you can be a fun teacher and make the job enjoyable for you and your students.

Discover New Things Together

While we have established that your primary role is that of an educator, nowhere does it say that you cannot engage in the joy of shared discovery with your students. Discovering non-academic things together can be a bonding experience for you and the students.

Preferably, let down your guard at the end of each lecture, humble yourself, and enjoy a few minutes of discovering each other together.

What's the latest in video games? Perhaps Jamie would like to share how he got his hands on the latest Smash Bros. Maybe Katie wants to tell you about the trip she and her parents took to Belize over the summer. You can initiate the sharing process yourself, telling them how you watched, let's say, the latest season of *Stranger Things* and enjoyed it.

Maybe a student in your class recently got their hands on a drone. Perhaps they want to share what the drone can do and how it can fly for an hour on a single charge of battery.

Take a genuine interest in what the students share with you. Give encouraging feedback whenever they tell you something and build upon what they've shared.

Add a Flair of Mystery to the Lessons

It's time to put on your Sherlock Holmes cap and add an element of mystery to the lecture. Treat it not as a traditional lecture but as a murder mystery or a role-playing game where the class has to come together and solve the clues to discover a hidden fact.

You can even use props to make things more exciting. Think dry ice for smoke, lasers for strobe lights, and colorful curtains to set a festive mood in the class.

Take a moment to enjoy the puzzlement and curiosity on the face of your students as they try to solve the mystery. Of course, the mystery shouldn't be so hard that they can't solve it. Assist them throughout and celebrate with them as they uncover the secret.

Laugh with Your Students

Laughter has its place within the classroom. It can be an excellent stress relief to lighten the mood and be goofy with the kids for a while. Make harmless jokes and share funny quips with the students as part of their lessons.

If you're coming up dry in the jokes department, you can always ask the class to share some with you. You'll be surprised to discover that the kids have a supply of completely new and funny jokes that we haven't heard before.

If you encounter a humorous situation in your life, you can share it with them as long as it is appropriate. Don't worry about sacrificing your sense of authority at the expense of indulging in humor with the students. Research has shown that authority stems from showing that you care about your students. Laughing with them is a brilliant way to show that you care for them.

Liven up the Lessons

Besides adding additional interactive learning measures to your lessons, such as experiments, demonstrations, and multimedia, you should liven things up in the classroom by encouraging your class to bring their creativity to the table.

If the syllabus has a Ray Bradbury short story, how about some fun reenactment where the kids play the role of Martians and astronauts? Maybe they want to perform a re-enactment of the Declaration of Independence, complete with costumes and toy muskets.

If the students get in the groove of the lesson, let them take the reins for some peer-to-peer learning. Sit back and watch as they collaborate in group discussions, debate, and find creative solutions to problems by coming together.

This stylistic shift where you and the students actively exchange ideas regarding a concept will create a fusion of learning that will liven things up in the classroom. Instead of delivering one-sided lectures, turn the lesson into a conversation. Talk to them as you would to a good friend.

If the kids want to improvise during a lesson, let them. Give them creative room to perform, learn, engage, and inspire themselves. When children feel they're in control of the situation, they become more adaptive to learning.

Use Social Media as a Tool

With the advent of TikTok, Instagram, Facebook, and Reddit, social media have transformed from just a social platform where people share their life to a tool through which people share specific interests such as their talents, their areas of academic expertise, and their hobbies.

From amateur kangaroo farmers and raft-building tutorials to how to dance like a Gen-Z, platforms like TikTok and Instagram contain an encyclopedia of information. Their usage extends beyond just social interaction online.

You can use social media to compliment your lessons by sharing relevant posts with the class in a multimedia presentation. You can discover what social media the kids use in your class. Additionally, you can go the extra mile by discovering what their favorite shows and videogames are.

Connect their games, shows, and activities on social media to their lessons through effective examples that demonstrate the theory you learn in action in those shows, games, and social media posts.

A lesson about magnetism and electricity can become an exciting discussion about hoverboards and how *Back to the Future* predicted that the future would have floating boards that operated through magnetism. Maybe even share a few snippets from the movie with the kids.

Similarly, find channels on social media that are relevant to information, such as wildlife channels, science channels, and educational channels, where information is presented in a fun, engaging, and informative manner.

These days, video games are another facet of social media just as much as the gaming industry. You can use the themes and mechanics of these games to demonstrate some lessons.

Use Real-Life Scenarios as Learning Opportunities

For this method, you'll have to discover your students' favorite hobbies. Ask them to write down all their hobbies, then narrow them down to the top three. Now use this information in your lessons to explain concepts.

Let's say one of their top hobbies is swimming. Kids love to swim and take part in swimming-based sports like water polo.

You can deliver a lesson on the properties of water within the context of swimming to capture their interest.

Keeping pets is another hobby that's bound to be in the top three. Explain how different mammals, birds, amphibians, and reptiles have specific characteristics from millions of years of evolution. Create examples from dogs, cats, rabbits, parrots, and turtles.

If sports cars and racing are another top pick, you can use this opportunity to teach them about inertia, momentum, velocity, acceleration, friction, and centripetal force. You can expand upon this topic by sharing the laws of thermodynamics, the properties of engines, and how aerodynamics factor in car racing.

You should invite the children to deliver a small lesson using their hobby. Trust your students that they have the critical skills to connect their hobby to the lesson.

Engaging them in topics that are directly related to them will make learning opportunities more impactful and helpful for the kids.

Go Beyond the Classroom

Your students need help in other facets of their life. If you want to go the extra mile, see what you can do for the students outside the classroom to help them achieve their potential.

If some students struggle with sports, maybe spend some time with them after school in the gym, where you can help them perfect their form. If a student is having trouble with playing instruments for a musical, stick around, encourage them, and if you know how to play the instrument, assist them in their lesson. Similarly, if the students are having issues putting on a play, help them get rid of nervousness and pre-performance jitters by getting them out of their comfort zone and letting them spread their creative wings.

Sometimes, students will come to you with issues unrelated to their school. They might come to you with some problems they're having at home, issues they're facing with bullies in school, or some hurdle they're facing regarding their mental health that they're too scared to share with anyone.

First, you must understand that it took great courage and trust to come to you with their issue. Now, do right by the students and help them with the problem they're facing. Make sure you offer the students ample guidance and assist them throughout the issue so they can trust you to come back to you again if they face a similar problem.

Through these methods, you can cultivate a relationship with your students where they trust you as an adult, confide in you as a friend, and look up to you as their guide. They will respect you, love you, and appreciate you. Later in life, whenever they achieve academic or career-related success, they'll always think of your positive impact on them.

Chapter 9: How to Add Movement into The Classroom for Greater Student Focus

"Keep calm and pretend this is on the lesson plan."

Student learning is a critical process that depends on many factors within and outside the classroom. For children aged five to ten years, variables such as classroom environment, syllabus, and the teacher's teaching methods are some of the important features that dictate how well they will learn.

One of these important issues is movement within the classroom. Research has shown that sitting at a desk for prolonged periods can hinder students' learning ability and lower their engagement within the class. And it's not just students that don't react well to sitting still for a long period; human beings are not wired to sit still in general.

In a research conducted by the students of Texas A&M University, they discovered that assigning standing desks to high school students boosted their functioning skills and improved their neurocognitive performance.

While the primary purpose of adding movement to the classroom is to improve the student's focus and learning ability, there's another major benefit: It's excellent for the kids' physical health. When they're young, kids have a natural and perfect posture for sitting. They sit up straight, with their backs against the chair. However, the drawback of prolonged sitting is that they gradually start slacking in their chairs. This forms into a habit, and by the time they're in their teenage years, their posture has suffered terribly. If you're a teacher, you will already have noticed this. Just compare a group of elementary school students with teenagers. You'll notice the posture difference right away.

What if we nipped this habit in the bud? What if we integrated movement in the classroom to benefit the students? This would help them stay alert and fresh in class while also helping them retain their natural sitting posture.

When you teach your students in this unconventional way, it will send a message that you care about them. It will let them know that you're invested in their learning. That's why you're going the extra mile. That's why you're trying something new with them. Not only will this create a bond of trust and respect between you and your students, but it will also make them learn   better.

Creative Ways of Adding Movement In Your Class

Whether you're a bit of a traditionalist or tech-savvy, there are several ways you can add movement to the class. You can get creative and create some of your own exercises that are relevant to your lessons, or you can take some ideas from here and try adding your mix to them.

Virtual and Augmented Reality

If there's one unobjectionable fact on the face of this planet, it's that kids love everything related to video games. Notice how they're still talking about the latest skins, weapons, and features in their games when they're at school. Look at their stationery items, their bags, and their clothes. They represent their favorite gaming franchises.

What if we could incorporate a bit of a videogame-related flair into the class? You don't have to do anything as drastic as installing PlayStations for the entire class. Think back to when you were a student. Whenever your teacher would roll in the trolley with the TV and the VCR, didn't you used to get excited?

There are so many tools online that let you craft your own images and scenes in VR. You can either utilize those tools or use some resources that are already available online. You can invest in a couple of VR goggles and have the students take turns with the lesson.

The possibilities are endless. From science lessons where you can have the students interact with the planets, galaxies, and stars in our solar system to social study lessons where you can run simulations of historical events for the kids to immerse in. VR and augmented reality have many applications you can use to add a fun movement to the class and have the kids learn innovatively.

Acting It Out

Elementary school students are especially fond of role-playing. An otherwise drab session about *Moby Dick* becomes an immersive maritime adventure where children can play the role of Ishmael, Captain Ahab, and even the whale. If a play is part of your syllabus with multiple characters, you can assign different characters to different students and let them interact with each other rather than sit and read the play. Encourage them to add their flair to the play or story and *become* the characters that they're playing.

You'll be surprised when exams show up at how well your students perform in the questions related to the study material. Acting it out engages all their different learning faculties, making them get the most out of the lesson. Drama and roleplay don't just have to be limited to English literature classes. You can let the students act out in history and social studies classes. Wherever there's a story, there's room to roleplay.

Nature Walks

There's always something new to learn during nature walks. From hiking trails to local treks around the hills or lake, there are flora and fauna that your students can learn to identify, wildlife that they can witness in their natural habitat, and fresh air that they can breathe out in the open. A simple nature walk around your schoolyard will suffice just as well. Your kids can grab a notebook and pencil and walk around the yard, looking for different varieties of plants and insects, listen to the sounds of nature and birds, and become more appreciative of the nature surrounding them.

Learning Related Games

There are so many learning games out there that it might get hard for you to choose which one's best for your students. From word-related games like Scrabble to cognition-related games like Build a Block, you have a wide array of options to choose from. These games will not only help the students become more collaborative but also add a touch of fun to the classroom with little to no expense.

Split the class into two groups and have them compete against each other in the form of quizzes, relays, and mock discussion sessions. This will also break the boredom in the classroom while rearranging the students and letting them move freely about the classroom.

Engage the Students in Your Lecture

Here, you will move throughout the classroom instead of the students. However, that's still just as beneficial as it will help the students remain alert and attentive to your lecture. If you're just delivering a lecture at the front of the class, students in the back might get bored or lose focus during the session. If you're constantly moving about the classroom, moving your way from front to back, the students' focus will constantly be on you and what you're saying.

Mini-Recesses

Award the high-performing kids in your class with a mini-recess where they can move about the classroom, take a break and go out into the hall to get a drink of water or stretch their legs.

It will motivate all the students to perform better. You can even randomly hand out the mini recesses to the students you feel need them most. If some students look tired or not focused enough, let them avail the mini-recess and become fresh so they can come back and participate with their complete potential.

Use the Gym or Playground for Problem-Solving

We're talking about math and science problems here. You know there are always specific math problems with x number of tomatoes and y number of watermelons? Take your class out into the gym or the playground. Substitute the watermelons for baseballs and the tomatoes for tennis balls and let the students visualize those problems. Similarly, you can use gym and playground apparatus to demonstrate how specific chemical reactions take place or how the laws of physics are universally applicable.

The idea of being in a gym or playground will appeal to the kids. It'll get them off their feet and make them interact with your planned lesson in a curious way.

Implement a Movement Policy

Introduce a policy that encourages kids to move as they learn. For example, if the kids have to go out to the drinking fountain, they should touch the ground after each step. If they want to sharpen their pencils, they should stretch their arms. If they want to answer or ask a question, they must stand up. Before the class is over, they have to make a lunge as they leave the classroom.

Gradually, you'll notice that these movements will become the students' habits and help them become more agile and stronger. It'll also ensure that they're alert during your class.

Ball-Toss

The ball toss is a fun idea for whatever class you're teaching. You have a ball at your desk at all times. During the lecture, you can toss the ball at one of the students to tag them. Now they must answer the question on the board or spell out a word. This will not only add an element of suspense to the class but also make the students remain focused. They'll keep focused on what you're teaching, always anticipating when you'll throw the ball next. Who knows whose turn is going to be?

Let's Measure it All

There will be a geometric element in your science or math class. Whenever that element comes into play, you can let the kids go around the classroom, measuring different things such as the chairs, tables, posters, pens, windows, and doors. Log their measurements in a chart for fun. Make up a reward system where you reward the students for the accuracy of their measurements.

Add Some Thrill with the Fitness Dice

Invest in a fitness dice. You can get them for cheap on Amazon or any online retailer. These dice have exercises on every side. Bring out the fitness dice during the class and have a random student roll the dice. The whole class must perform whatever the dice says, whether it's pushups or jumping jacks. Even short bursts of movement such as this can go a long way in making a big difference in their learning.

Creating a Snapshot

The theory behind this exercise is that your students form a physical snapshot of a lesson. They become still for a few seconds, the "snapshot" moment, so that their positions become an embodiment of an idea.

For example, if there's a lesson about different states of matter. A couple of students can become "liquid", some can become "solid", and others can turn into "gas" in a creative and visually captivating manner. You can even take a picture of them and stick it to the soft board for fun.

Students are very creative and are always ready for a chance to showcase their creativity. Letting them perform exercises such as creating a snapshot brings out their dormant creativity and allows them to become more confident in their capabilities.

The Benefits of Adding Movement in the Classroom

Maintaining student engagement by including various movements in the class will give you, the teacher, and your students many amazing benefits that will be beneficial to their learning and general health. This is much better than expecting the students to sit idly for an hour while passively listening to their teacher.

Efficient Learning

The hippocampus is the part of the brain that processes information while responsible for short-term memory and navigation. It takes the hippocampus some time to process the information while the student is learning something. Adding movement breaks to the class allows the students' hippocampus to process their information during the break.

When the student returns to the lesson, their brain can focus better.

Movement is not only important for information processing and retention; it also serves to help develop social skills among students. These skills are essential for comprehension and critical thinking.

Exercises and movements allow the body and brain to realign, helping students re-energize during the lesson.

A creatively delivered lesson incorporating fun movement is bound to be remembered for longer by the students than by a lecture that doesn't engage them.

It Creates Class Cohesion

By just introducing movement to the class, you will heighten your students' attendance and improve their performance in the class. It will allow them to build relationships and create empathetic concern for each other's wellbeing. Making your students interact through movement in the class will make them feel like they belong, therefore improving their self-esteem. When you let the students perform in the class, it will boost their communication and listening skills.

Most importantly, it will create a fun environment where students can laugh while they learn and be light-hearted during the lesson.

Since they will be actively enjoying their class, incorporating movement into the classroom will motivate them to perform better and improve their self-discipline.

It Gets the Blood Flowing

Around 90% of the oxygen in our body is stale until we take a deep breath, yawn, or move our bodies. Lack of fresh oxygen can result in a lack of focus, memory issues, and confusion during class.

Incorporating movement in the class will ensure that your students are getting fresh oxygen to keep them alert, focused, and vigilant.

Movement Creates Brain Breaks

Brain breaks are an integral part of learning. A typical brain break involves getting the students to move and allowing their blood and oxygen to flow to the brain. Small breaks allow the students to refocus their minds and better focus on their studies.

Brain breaks also affect a student's emotional states. As we already discussed, the hippocampus can only process so much information at once. Allowing students to take breaks lets them reset their hippocampus so that they can absorb more information.

The benefits of brain breaks include increased productivity, better comprehension, creative thinking, and a better ability to complete their tasks on time. Brain breaks let the students pay attention in class while increasing their efficiency and performance.

They're not just valuable for students; teachers also benefit from brain breaks. By coming up with creative ways to add movement in the class or including fun activities that break the monotony of the lecture, the teacher can strengthen their bond with the student. It lets the students know you're with them, not against them.

Chapter 10: How Personalized Learning Opportunities Can Boost Motivation

"I had a lot of teachers over the years who made a positive lasting impression, and I loved school. If I had to pick one teacher, it would be Mr. Whitman, my elementary school band teacher. He took time with each student as individual people and got to know what made them 'tick'. He was always positive and encouraging. He showed a passion for and dedication to the subject he taught." — Wendy, student.

Each learner has a unique capability for learning. Think about a classroom. While some students may have immediately understood the topics you taught them, others will still have questions. Some students leave the classroom as soon as the bell rings to signal the conclusion of the lecture, while others may still be having trouble understanding it. Other groups of students believed that the lecture was unnecessary because they had already grasped the material on their own and found the presentation boring.

As more research is being conducted into students' learning patterns, it's becoming evident that the one-size-fits-all approach is not the ideal approach to teaching. How does that relate to classroom management? A well-managed classroom is where all the students are equally involved in the lesson, all participating in the class with similar enthusiasm, and no student is left behind. In an ill-managed classroom, some students are learning, no doubt, but what about most of them? What of the rest who are not as studious, not as receptive to new concepts? Sooner or later, they will disassociate from the class and fall behind. This might cause them to rebel by creating disturbances and disrupting the learning process for the rest of the students.

However, there is an added dilemma here for the teachers as well. They cannot just always cater to the few high-achieving students. They have to take care of the entire class. Yet, they cannot stop the lecture to assist the one or two students who keep falling behind. The teacher has to remain vigilant of the learning pace of different students. It can become difficult to manage different students with varying capabilities in a group instruction-based lesson.

Teachers are now realizing that they need a flexible learning plan where they can implement personalized learning strategies within the classroom to make a real difference.

What is Personalized Learning?

Personalized learning is based on the premise that every student learns in different ways and at different paces. In this learning style, students get a learning plan based on their learning, what they've already learned, and what kind of skills and interests they possess.

The students participate in a collaborative process with their teachers to come up with long-term and short-term goals that they can achieve. The process of setting goals lets the students take ownership of their education.

Teachers ensure that the learning plans or the project-based learning methods align with the students' learning capabilities and the overall academic standards. The teacher monitors the student to ensure that the student demonstrates the skills they're expected to learn from their personalized learning plan.

Personalized learning takes the individual student's needs, interests, and abilities and tailors a learning module around them. Each student is given different instructions based on their learning characteristics.

The end goal of a personalized learning program is that the student reaches complete mastery of the topic by the end of the semester or school year.

Why Does Personalized Learning Work?

Learning is not a linear process. To grasp a single concept, a student has to integrate that concept with what they've learned so far. Sometimes, they have to unlearn something to relearn it with new parameters. A teacher cannot expect every student to learn one topic similarly.

When you create a personalized learning experience for the students, you allow them to get the right kind of education based on how they learn in a matter that interests them.

Granted, it will take more time than just delivering the same lecture to the entire class and moving on to the next lesson. Still, the long-term benefits of a personalized education program outweigh any disadvantages.

Benefits of a Personalized Education Program

When you introduce a personalized education program, you earn your students' trust and respect. Many of them won't say it to your face, but they *are* struggling with the lessons. They're either too afraid to say it or lack the confidence to confront their limitations in front of the entire class. By personalizing their education, you remove the burden from their shoulders and take it upon your own. These students will be grateful to you for making things easier for them. As a result, they'll put more effort into furthering their relationship with you and the classroom.

Students Will Learn More than Just Academic Lessons

Personalized learning gives a lot of freedom to the student to decide what kind of learning process suits them best. When they tackle a lesson with their specific skill sets, they become more confident in dealing with problems. They learn to tackle issues rather than run away from them.

When students share their goals and aspirations regarding the personalized learning program, they will develop motivation and self-reliance. They will develop self-advocacy skills when they determine what learning activities are best for them. When they self-assess their skills and learning requirements, they'll develop self-reflective abilities.

Learning at their own pace and in their own style will give them the autonomy required to cultivate confidence. It will also bring about joy in the learning process, motivating them to educate themselves further. It might just be a personalized learning program to you, but you might be helping a lost student decide on pursuing education at a higher level thanks to the interest you've fostered in them.

Students Will Improve their Knowledge Significantly

A study by the Gates Foundation discovered that introducing personalized learning to supplement math instructions improved the students' test scores from below the national average to exceeding the national average.

You're providing them additional material that goes beyond just what the school textbook provides. Instead of just delivering them a cut-and-dry lesson about a certain topic, you are providing them proactive means to interact with the lesson and learn at their own pace, in their own style. This might let them make discoveries in lessons that they wouldn't have made otherwise.

Let's run a scenario here. Edgar Allan Poe's works have long been a part of the English curriculum in many schools worldwide. Let's say that a few students have trouble understanding poetry. They don't get the point of poetry, they don't feel the need to understand what made Poe's work stand out from the rest of his contemporaries, and they don't feel the appreciation for the many poetic devices that Poe used and popularized.

Now, let's say that you introduced those students to the effects that Poe's works have on modern pop culture. From *PBS* docuseries to rap battles featuring Poe, there is so much supplemental material that you can introduce that lets the students engage with Poe's works. You have an opportunity at your hands to cultivate a love for the poet and poetry in general. Think *Dead Poet's Society* but for elementary school kids. At the end of the school year, you will not only have delivered the lessons to them but also made them fond of poetry. Now they know more than just what Poe was about; they know about different styles of poems, poetic devices and have a love for literature in general.

You Can Help Students Without Them Feeling Stigmatized

Students with specific weaknesses are always afraid that they will be classified in need of "special-ed." However, with the help of personalized learning, you can give them the support they need without them feeling inadequate.

You will be able to educate them without being subjected to peer pressure from other students, without worrying about lagging behind the class, and without ever feeling embarrassed when they get stuck in a lesson, thanks to personalized learning.

This is also a great chance for the teacher to fill in any knowledge gaps and bring all students up to speed.

Strategies to Implement Personalized Learning in Your Class

Since many personalized learning programs will be collaborative, you'll have more opportunities to create targeted teaching strategies. Let's look at some of them.

Tend To the Attentive One's First

There will always be students in your class who excel at the lesson. If it's math exercises, they'll be the ones who are done first. If it's a comprehension test, they'll be sitting idle before halftime, having completed their assignment. These students have been paying attention, learning the best they can, and have excellent performance.

However, while you're dealing with the rest of the class, you might be wasting these students' time. They might be sitting bored, thinking about what they're supposed to do next. You can give extra questions to them. They can be harder questions if you want. After all, we know that they can solve the simpler ones in record time. Give them something that engages them so that they don't sit idle. It's important that these students feel challenged; otherwise, they will not take the lesson seriously.

Similarly, if the whole class is reading and you notice that some students have read faster than the rest, you can put them in a group and discuss the contents of the upcoming chapters.

Personalized learning isn't just for the students struggling with the lessons. It's also for those more receptive than the rest of the students. It helps to pace them and let them stay focused on the subject while still being part of the class.

Utilize Ed-Tech to Empower Students

Leveraging modern technology to create customized learning plans for your students will empower them and make them interact with knowledge in fun, innovative ways. There are numerous resources, such as Khan Academy, dosomething.org, and IXL, where lessons are broken down into basics and taught innovatively to speak to students of different learning levels.

Creating online learning platforms such as forums and wikis can create a sense of collaboration between students where they can assist each other and participate in group activities at their own pace.

E-learning platforms that let you dynamically track and manage the progress and needs of your students will give you tangible data that you can use to craft personalized lessons for your students.

Game-based learning systems are another example that lets students learn at their own pace and have fun. Prodigy Math is a math game that is adaptive and curriculum-aligned. So far, it's helped more than 100 million students worldwide learn mathematics in a personalized way.

You can also opt for simpler tools at your disposal. Google Docs can serve as an excellent example here. You can group students and have them collaborate on the same doc. You can also check them from your computer, noticing how they perform.

Let the Students Participate in their Personalized Learning

Most lessons and lectures do not consider the student's preferences or interests. That's a major reason students lose focus during class and resort to breaking the rules.

If you flip the script and involve the students in creating a personalized curriculum based on their preferences, their interest, and their dominant skills, you'll notice that your students will develop more self-advocacy. They will pay more attention to the lessons since they had a role in crafting them. They will learn optimally.

Take university classes as an example. In universities, students can choose elective subjects and even pick majors. Computer science majors can opt for either web development classes or mobile development classes based on where their interests lie. Some might opt for cloud computing. Others who aren't interested in programming will choose networking and system administration. Since there's a variety to choose from, the students pursue the subject with greater interest.

You have to understand that for the students, this is probably the first time in their lives they're being offered some semblance of independence and self-reliance. Back at home, their parents take care of them. In the rest of the classes, they have to obey their teachers. In your class, though, they have the opportunity to voice their opinions and make themselves feel seen and heard.

From the perspective of self-growth, it's a fascinating step for them.

Realize Their Ambitions

Take some time to truly know them. Not the proverbial "what do you want to be when you grow up?", but something more profound. Understand what their hobbies are, what interests them, and what they do in their free time. Ask them what inspires them, what they wish to pursue further in life, and why they've chosen that particular field to pursue.

Don't just ask them about their ambitions, help them understand the meaning of their ambitions. When a student in your class tells you that they're interested in becoming an astronaut, encourage them with plausible explanations and steps that they can follow to pursue that dream. Tell them how there's groundbreaking work being done at institutes like NASA and SpaceX and how scientists are now trying to civilize Mars and set up colonies in space. Inspire an interest in their subject matter by sharing peripheral information about their ambition.

A student who loves to draw and wants to become an artist should be shown the portfolios of famous modern artists who have made fascinating strides in their careers. Introduce them to modern tech tools like drawing tablets and software like Photoshop so that they become more mesmerized by their ambition.

Kids with a creative flair should be encouraged to participate in creative exercises such as writing, dancing, role playing, and solving analytical puzzles.

If multiple students in your class share the same interest, group them together so that you can focus on them as a group.

Every child has an ambition. Some might not mention it because they think it's silly or too childish. Nurture them, boost their confidence, and encourage them to share their dreams. Do they want to swim with the dolphins and octopuses? A career in marine biology is an excellent choice for them. Do they want to play video games and do nothing else? Quality assurance as a game developer is a lucrative field where they can earn money from just playing games.

Whatever their ambitions are, it's important that you listen to them, realize them, and help them understand what they mean.

Once you've gathered information on all the students regarding their interests, passions, and ambitions, you can use that information to your advantage. You can craft lesson plans that target their interests. You can add real-life examples from their favorite things to make them more interested in the lesson.

Conduct an Aptitude Test

An aptitude test will be an irrefutable source of data that will show you what your students excel in, their weaknesses, and what they can improve on. Aptitude tests do not have to be strictly academic. They can have peripheral learning elements that will ensure that the test is not too jarring or boring.

Through this test, you will recognize patterns within your class. You'll understand what areas of deficiency you need to work on together. You'll learn about what general interest captivates your class as a whole. Now, with this data, you can create a personalized learning plan in a much more thorough way.

Chapter 11: Celebrating the Success of Your Students in Class

"My art teacher gave me encouragement to be curious and try different things with lots of praise no matter how things turned out." — Sherri, student.

Besides just being a teacher to the class, you're also their listener, organizer, manager, facilitator, mediator, and motivator. In my experience as a teacher, I have learned that one of the most important contributing factors to enhancing your students' success rate is motivating them to want to do better and helping them believe they can do well.

If you want your students to achieve academic prowess, you have to find ways to motivate them to tap into their potential and become the best version of students they can be.

A student's belief in their ability can lead them to great accomplishments. When you motivate struggling students, you can help them persevere and overcome their challenges.

In general, how many opportunities do students get in the course of their education to celebrate their academic achievements? Celebrating the success of your kids is one way to motivate them. It shows that you believed in them all along and were just waiting for them to succeed.

Students get caught up in stats and numbers in the form of report cards and test results, thinking that dictates whether they've succeeded or failed. The true value of education is intangible. It goes beyond just grades. Education is meant to shape the mind and spirit of a student and help them become a better person. As their teacher, you must help your students realize that life is more than test scores. Real success comes from hard work, persistence, and personal growth. Whenever you see your students working hard, growing, and persisting, that's an occasion for celebrating their success.

Even simple words of inspiration can go a long way in giving your students that much-needed boost.

10 Ways That You Can Celebrate Student Success in Class

In an otherwise indifferent world, your class can serve as a sanctuary, an oasis of inspiration where the students feel safe and acknowledged. Praising your students and celebrating their success will help make the classroom feel more like home for them.

Verbally Praise Your Students

Praising your students is the easiest way to motivate them and celebrate their success in class. Let's divide the students into three categories for the sake of this method. The first category is those of students who are struggling during a lesson. The second category is those students who perform averagely. The third category is those students who excel at the lesson.

A pep talk to the struggling students before a class quiz, or an assignment will help them overcome their fear of the task. After the quiz/assignment is done, praise them for how they have performed. Highlight the parts where they have performed well. Give them an encouraging talk about the parts where they struggled. Let them know you're in their corner and that together, they can get past that problem.

Now, with the average students, you want to motivate them so that they excel at the lesson. Introduce a little healthy competition between them and promise a reward to those who perform well. We'll discuss the reward part further on.

To the students working hard and performing optimally, praise them in front of the class. Acknowledge their hard work and use them as examples for the rest of the class.

You have to be as specific as possible when you praise individual students. Make sure that it's not just generic praise. Let the students know where they exceeded your expectations and how they impressed you. Add some eye contact and a hearty smile to make the gesture genuine.

The Wall of Fame

You can either make a section on the soft board or get a separate cork board for creating a custom wall of fame. You can decide upon the specific rules of the wall of fame with your students, but the gist is that it should celebrate the achievements of all the students in your class. Whenever some student does something great, they get their picture and name on the wall of fame.

Another variant on the wall of fame is to create a student of the week board, where the student who did the best in class that week has their name and photo displayed.

If you want it to be more inclusive, rather than a wall of fame, create a chart with every student's name and empty spaces in front of their name where you can pin color-coded stars depending on their achievements. For example, red stars can be academic achievement, green stars can be for hygiene, blue stars can be creative problem-solving, and orange stars can be for their collaborative spirit.

The purpose of these public displays of acknowledgment is to create an affirming environment where the success of the student is celebrated by the teacher and the rest of the students.

Sending a Note to Their Parents

While classroom-based praise establishes a good rapport between the students and the teacher, sending affirming notes that celebrate the student's achievements to their parents or guardian help the students interact with their parents regarding their school life.

Whether it's a note, an email, or a text to the student's parents or guardian, it will give the student a sense of accomplishment and pride that their teacher has taken the time to share their achievement with their parents.

It will also facilitate familial bonding between the student and the parents and lead to positive discussions about schoolwork, academic work, their challenges, and much more.

Most importantly, personalized notes from the teacher will make the parents and guardians feel like they're an integral part of their child's education journey. It will make them feel like they are part of the discussion regarding their child's learning.

They will be further encouraged to visit the school and talk to you about different school-related matters. Sending notes to their parents or guardians is an excellent way of opening a communication channel that will ultimately benefit the student.

Giving Them Incentives in the Classroom

Children love performing well in front of their peers. It's not only a great motivator but also an excellent opportunity for praising and celebrating them. Consider a reward system or a celebratory goal that unifies the students in their motivation to work harder. Let's say you implement a class reward system as a big jar. Add a change to the jar whenever a student performs well or does something splendid. At the end of the session, week, or school year, you can break the jar and treat the students to a nice party with the money in the jar.

You can also create a competition where you will only give the prize if the median score exceeds a certain number. This will motivate the students to help each other achieve high results on the test. When they succeed, celebrate in the form of a small party or by giving out award ribbons to the students.

If you want, you can create a raffle for the students that may depend on their academic achievement. The high performers will get tickets that will be put in the raffle box. At the end of the week, you can take out a lucky winner and give them a small prize or certificate.

Student-oriented incentives in the class create a sense of competition and healthy rivalry, as both serve as excellent motivators.

Peer Recognition Activities

While praise and encouragement from the teacher are integral to student growth, getting recognition from their peers is just as important. To facilitate such recognition, you can arrange an event where the students participate in highlighting the strengths of each other in class.

One example that comes to mind is the activity called "strength circle." All the students form a circle in the strength circle and have envelopes with their names on them. They pass the envelopes to their right. Every student writes down a strength of their peer in their envelope and then hands it over to the next person in the circle. By the time the rotation has finished, every student in the class has some form of praise from every other student in their envelopes.

Besides creating camaraderie, it will strengthen their bonds and allow them to celebrate with each other.

Teacher's Assistant for the Day

Reserve the role of teacher's assistant for the day for the student who performs the best in class that day. Students love to get some form of monitor role in the class. You can let them help you take notes, wipe the board, gather papers from the class, run errands, and monitor the class should you go out.

Make sure you eventually let everyone be an assistant for the day so that every student feels like they have an equal shot at this position. It'll further motivate them to perform better, giving them more opportunities to be your assistant.

Sharing Their Success Online

Make sure you get the consent of your students and their parents before sharing anything online. Once you've been given consent, you can share your student's success on the school's social media pages and blog.

You can even set up an Instagram account designated just to share your students' success stories. Every week or every other day, you can upload a post that celebrates the accomplishment of one of your students, along with a blurb that highlights what they have achieved.

This is not just an excellent way to inspire your students, it also serves as a platform where the parents and guardians of your students can come together and participate in the celebration of their children. Furthermore, you have created something the students and their parents can share with their friends and relatives.

Hold Award Ceremonies Often

These award ceremonies differ from the school's end-of-semester/school year ceremonies. Your award ceremonies should be centered around which student has improved the most, which student has achieved great academic strides, and which student has shown personal growth.

You can invite other teachers, parents, and school board members to these ceremonies to give them a more official feeling.

Certificates

Certificates of achievement are tangible proof that the student performed well. When you hand them out in your class, you will be giving them something that they can pin on their wall at home, show their relatives, or even use later on when they apply for higher education, scholarships, or prep schools.

Certificates are easy to make as they can be printed and filled in quickly.

Showcasing their Work in the Classroom

Let your students be proud of their work by showcasing it in a visible spot in the classroom. You can either set up a space for their work on the soft board or create a separate section on one of the walls where you can pin up their reports, creative projects, essays, or assignments. Make sure that you don't clutter that space too much. A creative way to keep the showcase fresh and active is by updating it every other week. This will let all the kids see their work on the showcase over the school year.

The Benefits of Celebrating Your Students' Success

These celebrations aim to motivate your students. Effective praise can consistently improve their skills. To make the praise genuine, it should be sincere, specific, and realistic.

You will be building their confidence over the school year with your praise and celebration.

There is an essential connection between effort and achievement. Celebrating your students makes them realize there's a fundamental relationship between making an effort and reaping its rewards.

Lastly, you become the teacher that they need. You put yourself in the ideal position to be their friend, role model, and someone whom they can trust.

Chapter 12: Parent Connection Strategies to Build Powerful Relationships

"A good education can change anyone. A good teacher can change everything"

Think of your students' parents as someone on your team who can work outside the classroom. The parents are your students' safe space. They're someone who's always in their children's corner. Most children are very close with their parents. When students see that you, their teacher, are also close with their parents, they will be inclined to trust you.

Successful students are often backed by the efforts of their parents. Those parents are involved with their children's homework, assignments, and supplemental learning. They're invested in the learning process. Engaging those parents and letting them know how their children are performing will create more convenience for you and your students.

Parents are more inclined to trust a teacher with their child's learning who takes the step to form a relationship with them and nourish that relationship throughout the school year.

First-time parents whose eldest children are your students will naturally be more curious and concerned about how their kid is doing in class. You'll recognize them in parent-teacher meetings by the frequency of their questions and genuine concern for their child's well-being in the class.

You must have a powerful relationship with the parents of your students. Let's discuss some strategies you can use to form a strong bond with them.

Greet Them Warmly

Whenever you meet them, greet them warmly and smile at them. Remember, most parents only meet with their kid's teachers occasionally, so you must ensure that all those interactions are positive, warm, and friendly. The impressions they get from those short encounters can last a long time.

Engage in healthy small-talk. Don't just talk to them about what's happening in the class. Ask them how they're doing, how work's going, and if they have any fun plans for the weekend. Tell them a bit about yourself. It's important that you do this. When you share details about yourself, you'll create an image in their minds that you're a living, breathing person, not just a classroom teacher.

A simple, friendly greeting can lead to great strides in forming a relationship with them. When you smile at them, shake their hands warmly, and pat them on the shoulder, they'll see you as a friendly and approachable figure.

Learn Their Names

Get acquainted with the parents on a first-name basis. This will require some extra bit of work from you. You'll have to attend the students' sports events, competitions, and exhibitions. After all, there must be somewhere other than a parent-teacher meeting where you should meet them. What better place than inside the school while parents attend an event?

Learn their name and address them by their first names. It's an easy and effective way to establish a positive relationship with them. It shows them that you took the time to learn things about them and that you care about them. Parents know you have an extensive list of names to memorize with so many students. It will make them feel important and appreciative when you go the extra mile of remembering their name.

Soon, they'll start to consider you as a friend, not just a teacher.

Inform Them of Your Intentions

Whenever you get a chance to meet the parents, inform them of your intentions. Let them know that you want to collaborate with them to create an environment both within the school and at their home where the students can learn their best.

Talk to them about the various efforts you're making in the class and what programs you have in mind for the students that you think will help them tap into their potential.

Let them know that you are very much invested in the students and want the best for them. When the parents see this sincerity coming from you, not only are they going to respect you, but they're also going to feel very safe and confident about their choice of school. They're going to feel happy about their children being in your class.

You can share some tidbits with them, some special events that happened, and describe the daily challenges that come with teaching.

Communicate Often

You should be proactive in communicating with the parents of your students. Ideally, you should provide them with a weekly report of what happened in the class and how their kid learned something, overcame a challenge, or struggled with some subject matter. You shouldn't wait for the parents to reach out to you. Instead, you should take the first step.

Besides the monthly parent-teacher meetings, you should communicate with the parents through email and texts. Share details about their child with them. Ask them what their child likes, what they want, and how they perform in other aspects of life outside school.

Whenever a child accomplishes something substantial, share that detail with the parents to keep them in the loop.

In the beginning, it might take some effort to get the ball rolling, but soon you'll find that the parents will reciprocate and communicate with you with equal enthusiasm. They'll become invested in their child's education through your communication.

Phone Calls

Sometimes, it might be difficult for some parents to make it to school due to their hectic routine. Maybe both parents have day jobs that they depend on and cannot leave to come to school. Make sure that those parents aren't excluded from the discussion. You can ask your student for their parents' phone numbers and contact them via call.

Busy parents, especially parents who are balancing multiple jobs and juggling different responsibilities, will appreciate that you're doing your best to communicate with them. It might be best to talk to them after school hours when both you and they are free to talk.

Feel free to share the developments of their child in the class. If there is positive news, share it with them and let them know their child is doing a great job. If the student is struggling, emphasize to the parents that the kid needs additional help. Extend a helping hand to them so that they know they have a friend out there who cares for the well-being of their kid.

Lead With Good News

All the parents are concerned with how their child is doing in the class. They're eager to hear any positive news. They're investing their time and money by sending the kid to school, and they have hopes and aspirations for their child.

So, whenever you meet them, whether in a meeting, in an informal manner, or on a call, lead with good news to lift their spirits.

Every kid has something good about them. They each have some special abilities and characteristics; find those. Share them with the parents. They want to know how their kid is doing. You must adhere strictly to this rule.

Leading with positive news creates a communication channel where the parents can trust you and can confide in you about any issues regarding their child.

Get a Translator

There are many diverse students from different backgrounds. Their parents might not speak English as their first language. Don't let this create a barrier between you and them. Get a translator to make the communication easier. If you can't find a translator, you can let the student help with translating.

Even though they might not speak the language, those parents still understand what goes inside the school. They're just as concerned for their kids as other parents. You earn their trust and respect when you help them participate in the discussion.

Pay Attention to Your Language

This pertains to both your body language and your verbal language. There are many different kinds of families that children belong to. Some kids might be children of single parents. You must be mindful of the relationship status of the children's parents. Don't assume they're married or single unless they explicitly tell you. Rather than refer to them by any pronouns, try to use their names in the conversation. It's more personable.

Your body language conveys a subliminal message to them. Friendly gestures, firm handshakes, and a comfortable posture will make the parents comfortable in your presence.

Whenever you ask them questions, don't imply anything, and don't assume things on your own. It's better if the questions are open-ended. Sometimes, parents might not want to share details they're uncomfortable with. Respect that and move on to other questions.

Let the Parents Talk

This is more of an extension of the previous point. To truly understand the parents, you must let them talk first and share things with you. This will give you a clearer image of who they are.

They know a lot about their children. Hear their concerns, let them talk about the issues they're facing, and acknowledge what they're saying. Then, they'll also want to share details about their kid with you.

Ask questions between their statements to show that you're paying attention to what they're saying. Build upon what they're saying so that you can carry the conversation forward.

Ask Questions About Their Child

If you want to know more about your students, there's no better source than the parents. Ask them about the child. Let the parents share their insights with you. "What does the child like to do outside of school?" or "Who are some of the special people in her life?", "What was Tommy like as a little boy?" are some examples of questions that you can ask to get a better picture of the child.

It demonstrates that you're interested in knowing your students. It also gives the parents a platform to talk about their child. Many parents don't have other people to talk to about their children. Their child's teacher is an important person who cares for their child. The parents *want* to tell you things about the kid so that they can facilitate you in teaching their child in the best way you can.

Encourage Parents to Show Up for Meetings

Parent-teacher meetings are a vital part of your student's school life. For most parents, it's the only time they can come to the school and get feedback on how their child is performing. If you notice that some parents don't show up for the parent-teacher meetings, send them a note or a letter and encourage them to attend the meetings so that you can discuss their child's progress with them.

Creating Volunteer Opportunities for Parents

Many parents want to be involved in their child's school life but don't know how to do that. For those parents, you can create volunteering opportunities where they can come and assist you with planning class events. They show up for the meetings and attend the events, but they still want to do more.

These are just some of the strategies you can use to form a positive bond with the parents and guardians of your students. In the long run, it will help establish you as a teacher who goes the extra mile for their students. It will help nurture a bond between the parents and their children. Most importantly, you invest in the child's education when you meet the parents.

Chapter 13: Common Teaching Mistakes to Avoid

"My most influential horse trainer was kind, clear, and consistent, but the most striking thing was that whenever I made a mistake, he apologized for not explaining it to me well enough and explained it better. In other words, he wouldn't let me think I had made any mistakes." —Amanda, student

As with any profession, teaching also comes with many challenges that make it difficult for new teachers to navigate their profession without making a few mistakes. It should be noted that these mistakes are not intentional and do not speak for your ability to teach. More experienced teachers with some years of experience under their belts have already faced these mistakes and have learned to minimize them to create a more cohesive classroom.

Common teaching mistakes can create class discord and contribute to poor classroom management. It can also break the relationship between the student and the teacher by adding hostility, mistrust, and even animosity between each other.

A well-managed classroom is one where the teacher knows what problems to avoid and what mistakes not to make. Luckily, with my years of experience as an educator, I can help you navigate that territory and show you the common errors and what you can do to avoid them.

Rushing the Lesson

It's in no one's interest to rush a lesson. You might feel the need to hastily go over the contents of the lecture because of a shortage of time or to tick all the boxes in a checklist about what you've done. Doing so creates a very tense environment in the class where the students *fear* that they won't learn anything adequately. It creates a stressful situation for them where they struggle with the lesson regardless of whether they have a firm grasp over it.

It strains the relationship between the teacher and the students because the students perceive that the teacher is more concerned with going through the syllabus's topics than with them. When a teacher rushes a lesson, the learning part of the class suffers.

Sure, some of the students might be able to keep up with you, but the rest will quickly lose focus of what you're teaching them. They will engage in misbehavior and frivolity in class because they deem their time wasted.

It also conveys that the teacher has no interest in the subject and that they're just trying to make it through the day to get their paycheck at the end of the month. The more astute students of your class will quickly realize this, and sooner or later, word of your ineptitude will spread throughout the school.

You should be able to manage the schedule and the syllabus side by side. Before the start of the session, distribute the contents of the syllabus all over the calendar equally and allocate special time for trickier topics. Go over the subject with a more experienced teacher, and don't be afraid to ask for their help in this regard. Let them show you the ropes and learn how they manage to teach the lessons within the limited time.

Not Communicating Expectations Clearly

A surefire way to confuse all the students is to miscommunicate your expectations. What are the goals and takeaways that the students need to achieve by the end of the class? Do they know that, or are they just here to pass the time and listen to your lecture? Is there a coherent structure to the lessons, or are they just expected to learn the contents on their own back home?

What are some of the ramifications of poor performance? What are the rewards of performing well? What do you expect from the students?

Make sure that your expectations are clear and realistic. Rather than burden the students with a load they cannot bear, go over the course with them on the first day and share what you think is the ideal strategy for learning the subject. Let them know that there will be certain elements that are harder to grasp than the rest and that you and them will work together to overcome those tricky topics.

Set up the ground rules for discipline early in the session so that the students understand that you will monitor their behavior and assess their performance throughout the school year.

Being Inconsistent

You are a human being just like any other person out there. Teaching is one facet of your life. You go through the motions for the rest of your day just as everyone else does. You have to face some hardships, overcome troubles, pay the bills, manage relationships, deal with your family, and so forth. All of that translates to varying energy levels on different days.

An inexperienced teacher might overzealously deliver the greatest lecture in the history of the subject one day. The next day they might not even deliver a lecture and let the class read from the book. They might scold the entire class in one lecture and appear rational and calm in the next one. One week they'll be high-fiving the kids over a successful class performance, and the next week they'll be completely alienated from what the students are doing.

Inconsistency in your energy, your teaching methods, and your behavior in the class will create a very disruptive, unexpected, and confused environment in your class. The students will not know whether to look up to you as a role model or fear your unpredictability. They will be apprehensive when approaching you about a problem regarding the subject, not knowing whether you will encourage them or criticize them.

Remember what we talked about at the start of the book? Set your energy on the first day of school and consistently follow through every day with the same energy level. That's what you should do. Even when you're feeling tired or down, ensure you present yourself to the students properly. On days when you're chipper than usual, pace yourself and be consistent with your energy for the rest of the session.

You must pick an energy level that's most natural to you. You don't want to be inauthentic. Be yourself and be consistent.

Not Establishing Relationships

A new teacher might feel that forming a bond with students is not important. They might just be focused on delivering the lesson's contents without investing in the students, reading the room, and engaging the class.

This will convey to the students that the teacher does not care about them. Just as the teacher is indifferent to them, they too will become indifferent to the teacher and abandon any efforts of learning.

From the first day of class, start forming a relationship with every student. Be personable with them. Interact with them.

Engage in light-hearted conversation with them that doesn't relate to what's happening in the class.

Also, form a relationship with their parents, as discussed in the previous chapter.

You might only teach these students for just one year, but they will carry your lessons with them for the rest of their lives. Your relationship with these students will inadvertently shape them for better or worse.

Focus on cultivating organic, natural, and gradual relationships with your students. Let the relationships mature for the academic year. Remember why you're doing it. The relationship with the children is an investment in their learning process.

A teacher with a healthy relationship with their students will have a much more organized and managed classroom than a teacher who doesn't have a relationship with their students.

Not Intervening or Waiting Too Long to Intervene

All your students will struggle with something at one point or another in the academic year. Some might be struggling with the lessons, while others might struggle to form a relationship with the rest of their class. Some kids might come from troubled homes. Others might be having trouble with bullies in school. Students face many problems throughout the school year. A good teacher is innately aware of these problems because of their working relationship with the students.

A good teacher also ensures they intervene at the right time and solve their students' problems. They ensure that the student is facilitated and assisted in any way possible.

Take academics, for example. They're the prime responsibility of the teacher. If you notice that a student is not taking to the lessons like the rest of the class, it should be your priority to assist them with the lesson as soon as possible.

Similarly, if there's an issue between two students in your class, ensure that you help them resolve it and avoid any kerfuffle.

Keep an eye out for troubling signs of psychological problems among the students. There might be a serious underlying cause for the students' symptoms. Investigate and get to the root of the problem. Involve other figures in the issue, such as other teachers, the principal, and the parents.

It is the mark of a great teacher that they recognize an issue and nip it in the bud.

Going Big Too Quickly

New teachers sometimes over-ambitiously decide to completely disrupt the status quo and teach in a new format. They might feel inclined to start with the toughest concepts first, thinking that tackling the hardest things will make the rest of the school year easier.

Going big too quickly overwhelms the students and detracts them from learning.

Whatever measure you want to take, you should do it gradually. For example, if you want to rearrange the classroom, you should do it after consulting a few fellow teachers, reviewing the pros and cons, and finally implementing the changes over a while rather than all at once.

If you know the subject is tricky and has tough elements, don't overestimate the classroom's intelligence and tackle the hardest bits at the start. Build up to them. Break down the topic into easily digestible parts so that every student feels like they've learned the lesson.

Take feedback from the students at the end of the class. Involve them in the lesson planning. Hear what they have to share with you. And remember, slow and steady wins the race.

Using Negative Language

Students in the age range of five to ten have very impressionable and delicate minds. Every single word that you utter has a special meaning to them. Affirmative responses boost their confidence. Praise serves to make them happy and more motivated. Stern and negative language break their spirits. It instills fear in their hearts and demotivates them from learning.

Using negative language can carry several psychologically adverse effects that tarnish a child's emotional and mental growth. Discouraging them, admonishing them in front of the rest of the class, and using phrases like "bad," "stupid," "idiotic," "poor performance," "silly," and "crazy" are not only psychologically destructive but also a very bad practice to conduct as a teacher.

Negative language makes the students abhor coming to the class. It creates tension between you and the students. Rather than forming a relationship with you, they will learn to distance themselves from you and not pay any heed to whatever you're saying in class.

Using sarcastic remarks, disparaging the questions they ask, and shunning them from participating in the class ultimately disrespects the students and hurts their feelings. It also affects their performance in class. At best, it shows that you are indifferent to them; at worst, it shows that you bear them ill will.

By default, the kids look up to you and eagerly await what you have to teach them, share with them, and discuss with them. It's almost a sacred bond you should nourish and cherish rather than disrespect by using negative language in class.

Playing Too Much of a Lead Role

Of course, leading the class is part of your job designation, and it's a large part of what you will do in the class. However, playing too much of an authoritative lead role will not give the students a chance to express themselves. It's not a one-person show. Without you initiating the lecture, the students cannot start learning.

The students want to participate in the class. Give them a chance to do that. Often, open up the floor for discussions and stress the importance of student input.

Teaching is a two-way street. You have to get your students to participate in the class, join in the discussion, ask questions, and learn in more than one way. It's a common mistake for new teachers to be over-enthusiastic and take up too much time at the center stage.

Pause often during the lecture so that students have a chance to ask any questions.

Being a Passive Teacher

A passive or lazy teacher quickly disinterests the class in the lesson by resorting to some terrible teaching practices. They might ask the class to copy down notes from the board. They might teach from pre-made, downloaded slides. They might not deliver the lecture in its entirety.

A lazy teacher might read from preparation notes while they're teaching. Even if the topic happens to be an exciting and fun one, they will turn it into the drabbest and most boring presentation that will put off all the students.

Just as the students can detect if a teacher is disrespectful to them, they can also notice when a teacher is passive and lazy. It makes them feel helpless when the person who was supposed to guide and teach them does not perform their job optimally.

To avoid becoming a passive teacher, prepare your lectures beforehand and review your notes before coming to class. Engage the class in the lesson. Participate in a question-and-answer session. Move throughout the class while delivering your lesson, and use multimedia presentations during your classes. Help the students grasp the topic by delivering the lecture thoroughly.

The students will be intrigued if you show interest in the lesson.

Asking the Question, "Do You Understand?"

This is another common mistake that most teachers just starting out make. Most students will never give an honest answer when you ask them if they understand. Even if they don't understand, they'll nod and say yes to avoid embarrassment in front of the class. Some students are just too shy to show their ignorance. Instead, they opt to remain quiet.

Rather than ask, "do you understand?", go over the lesson a couple of times, emphasizing the important bits, and let the class ask questions after the session. If you feel like a student is struggling, talk to them after class, when they're alone, rather than confront them in front of the entire class.

Not Being Consistent About the Rules

Rules are the cornerstone of a well-managed classroom. It conveys a horrible impression to the students when you set rules on the first day of class and then fail to follow through on them throughout the rest of the year. What's worse is that it creates a disruptive environment in the class. The mischievous kids take it as an opportunity to do whatever they want and get away with it.

A good way to tackle this mistake is to set reasonable rules. Rather than many rules, come up with a limited number that is easy to implement throughout the school year. Keep a copy of the rules with you at all times and consult them frequently to ensure everyone follows them.

Working Too Hard

Teaching is a job that often requires hard work and borderline superhuman skills to manage the entire class daily. If you push yourself too hard and don't ask for assistance from your colleagues, you're going to burn out. You mustn't let the problems in the classroom affect your emotional well-being and your home life.

Teaching has the highest turnover rate of any profession out there. It's because most teachers work too hard and burn the candle on both ends, not realizing that they're doing it at the expense of their mental health.

Take frequent breaks. Once at home, relax and leave the problems of school behind. If you're stuck with a certain issue, don't be afraid or hesitant to ask for help from your colleagues. Make sure you balance your work life with your home life. Enjoy time with your friends and family, and make sure that you set out some time in your daily schedule to unwind and relax so that you can go to school tomorrow and start afresh.

Chapter 14: Maintaining Discipline and Helping Challenging Students

"My best teacher would have been my music teacher. He managed to control the whole class, even the naughty boys, by immersing everyone in music. He found the type of music they liked, and he used it to their benefit. He was the kindest and most compassionate man with a lovely, gentle manner. He was no walkover; he had boundaries, but he was not unkind to anyone, and everyone respected that." —Debbie, student.

Classroom management relies upon discipline as the foundation on which other elements such as personalized learning, creative seating arrangements, and integrating movement within the class all rely upon. Discipline is the most fundamental aspect that needs to be maintained for the students to learn in a conducive environment.

Setting proper classroom rules is vital for the order in class. Rules are essential for encouraging the best behavior from your students. Discipline is how the students learn classroom etiquette, understand what their responsibilities are and what you expect from them. Establishing understandable, value-based rules in the class can instill positive behavior in the students and is critical for their growth and development.

Setting Up the Rules

How can you ensure that the students follow and respect the rules? How can you develop rules that aren't too strict or unfair to the students? You can always involve the students in making the rules with you. When they're directly involved in the process, they will not constantly question the value of each rule.

Establish Rules that The Class Will Actually Follow

That's it, that's the key to establishing rules in the class. Make rules you're certain the class will follow because they're reasonable rules. Some instances of these rules can be:

1. Being punctual. It's one of the best habits you can cultivate in students. Always being on time is essential to ensure that the classroom runs smoothly. This is a rule that you can

demonstrate in addition to laying out. You can make yourself an example to the kids by coming to class on time every day.

2. Respect everyone. Add a subtitle to this rule that says, "treat others the way you want to be treated." Inform the kids that this means that they have to respect each other and you. Emphasize that there's a zero-tolerance policy for rude behavior, bullying, or negative attitudes toward each other. In addition to respecting each other, students should be encouraged to be kind and help each other whenever possible.

3. Finishing work on time. It's a simple rule that fosters punctuality and timeliness in the students. Unless the teacher provides an extension, every assignment and test should be submitted on time. This will teach the students to respect deadlines, a skill that will serve them well as adults. You can enforce this rule by giving late assignments a lower score to encourage punctuality.

4. Keeping the classroom clean. The classroom is supposed to be the kid's second home. It's the place where they spend the most time outside of their homes. This rule highlights the importance of keeping everything tidy and discouraging students from littering the classroom with food, supplies, and paper. Encourage the students to work together at the end of class to clean everything and put things back into their places.

If someone has made a mess, it should be their responsibility to clean it up.

5. Don't disturb other students; raise your hands if you have questions. Tell them that raising their hand to ask a question is one of the basic rules of elementary school. This rule will stop students from chatting with each other during class and help focus their entire attention on your lesson.

6. Asking permission before leaving the class. If a student needs to do something outside the class, or visit the bathroom, they should use the hall pass or ask your permission before they leave.

7. Actively participate in the classroom. Any form of classroom-related activity is an integral component of the learning process. Students should be advised to take part in these events.

8. Respect each other's property. Let the students know that they shouldn't steal each other's belongings and that they have to ask permission before borrowing something. Similarly, anything that belongs to the classroom is the school's property and should be used as such.

Posting the Rules

These rules should be posted where they are visible to everyone. You can pin them up on the soft board, tape them to a wall, or paste them behind the door in case you keep the door closed during classes.

A Zero-Tolerance Policy

Every rule should have a zero-tolerance policy. Those who break the rule should pay the fine or face the repercussions. Even though you, as their teacher, have a friendly rapport with everyone in the class, you should also have a complete non-emotional and non-judgmental attitude while enforcing the rules. This lets the students know that you're strict and adamant when it comes to the rules.

Follow Through Every Time

As discussed in the previous chapter, not following the rules every time is a common mistake that new teachers make. That's why we made rules that are easily enacted. You should ensure that whenever someone breaks a rule, they're disciplined at once. Don't play favorites with the students. Whoever breaks the rules should also face the consequences.

The Punishment Should Be Logical

The students need to realize that there's a reason behind the punishment, that it's not there to berate or insult them. If someone makes a mess with art supplies, make that student clean the mess up and put the supplies back in the closet. If a kid is making a lot of noise or disturbing their peers, giving them a time-out tells the entire class that if anyone disturbs the classroom's environment, they will be given a time-out.

Make Up a Strike System

Give the rule-breaker three strikes. Tell them that the first strike is a warning. The second strike will result in a time-out. The third strike will result in sending a note to their home or making them visit the principal's office.

Never Punish the Whole Class

If a few students are making a mess or creating a disturbance, never punish the entire class because of them. The punishment should be reasonable and specific to those who have broken the rules.

Keeping Track of Discipline

Let the class know early on that you're going to keep track of their discipline. You can keep track of student misbehavior in your notebook or on your computer. This creates transparency between teachers and students.

This data is useful. Depending on how you deal with the rule-breakers, the trend in the data will show that the students are much more disciplined as the school year progresses.

Look out for the students who are making more trouble than the others. There's an underlying problem there. Misbehavior and trouble are just a symptom of the problem. Find out what that problem is.

For the more frequent troublemakers, you must get in touch with their parents and convey your concerns to them.

As you work on the students who need help, are struggling with the rules, and are stubborn in their ways, you'll notice that gradually, they'll stop misbehaving and start complying with the rules. If the disciplining techniques are reasonable and not humiliating, your discipline tracker will show a downward trend in student misbehavior.

Additionally, you can share with your students that their performance in the class will also affect how you grade their assignments, mid-terms, and finals. This will make them more accountable for their behavior.

As you track the discipline of your students, encourage and congratulate those who are performing better now. Let them know that your discipline was nothing personal.

Make sure you have a manageable and organizable method of tracking their discipline. The simplest and most convenient way is using a spreadsheet program like MS Excel.

If the student is facing a serious underlying problem, you and your colleagues can come together and take measures to resolve those issues. If you can get other teachers in the school to participate in creating a discipline tracker, you can share your progress with them. You can also go over different methods to discipline the troublesome kids creating trouble in their class.

The purpose of tracking their discipline is not to admonish the kids. You should not use this tracker to embarrass a student in public. Its purpose is to establish a method to minimize discipline issues in the class. It is so that you can develop a strategy to find the root cause of the issues and solve those problems.

Do's and Don'ts of Disciplining

Disciplining is just a means to an end. The purpose of disciplining the students is to create an organized and well-managed classroom where students can learn freely and participate in educational activities without any disturbances.

When disciplining a child, you should never show anger or frustration with them. This should be clear from the get-go. It's not personal. It's a mechanism put in place to ensure that everyone behaves according to the rules. When someone breaks the rules, deal with them in a non-emotional manner. Correct them and move on.

When dealing with rule-breaking consequences, it can be tricky to keep emotion out of the mix. If someone breaks a rule for the first time, calmly tell them they're getting a warning. Naturally, you'll feel some anger, but you must never let that anger show. It's harmful to the students.

Despite how often a student breaks a rule, you should never label them negatively. At their age, it's difficult to keep up with the rules. It's even more difficult when, due to their misunderstanding, they get labeled as something that they're not. You can do some psychological damage if you label them something derogatory. It will lead to a huge dip in their self-confidence and make them the subject of mockery from the rest of the class.

You need to ensure that when disciplining students, you never antagonize them. It would be very unprofessional to treat them differently in class after discipline. Your primary position regarding a student should always be a friendly one. When you've disciplined them, go back to that position.

Physical punishment is a huge no. You should never physically assault a student in the class. Not only can you physically damage their body, but you're also going to potentially create a lot of trouble for the rest of the students, the school, and yourself.

When a student has been disciplined, talk with them at the end of the class, where you discuss what they did and why they needed to be disciplined. You shouldn't resort to using a loud, scolding voice, as that's counterintuitive to what you want to achieve.

The goal of discipline is to ensure that the student realizes their mistake, understands that there's a mechanism in place where they'll get punished for making a mistake, and refrain from repeating it. It should never devolve into clashing egos or doling out punishment for just the sake of punishment. Just as you teach your students to be kind, you, too, should be kind to them, especially when they're difficult.

When a student gets a third strike, it's time to talk to their parents. Now, you must never scold or criticize the child in front of their parents as it will further strain the relationship between them and create animosity between you and the student.

Enhancing Communication and Collaboration

When you work with empathy as your primary tool, you will do wonders in the discipline department. Try to get the student to see things from your perspective. Communicate with them and let them know that when they break a rule or create a disturbance, it upsets the flow of the entire class and makes it difficult for the students to learn and the teacher to teach.

Encourage the students to self-regulate when it comes to enforcing the rules. Yes, you will monitor them all the time, but it will show the students that you have confidence in them and that you're letting them self-regulate their behavior. It will make the students trust you *because* you're trusting them.

You will discover that communication is one of the key elements in minimizing discipline issues. Even the most challenging students in your class will reduce their mischief if you establish a non-confrontational rapport. It will help them develop empathy for you and the rest of the class. Having a rapport with them will make it easier for them to confide in you about any trouble they're having. You can also rationalize and reason with them regarding their issues.

How To Minimize Discipline Issues

If you are managing your classroom well, there will be minimal discipline issues as it is. By utilizing techniques such as personalized learning, you will already be making sure that every child participates in the lesson in a way that is most helpful to them.

However, if there are still discipline issues, here are some ways to minimize them.

Stand Next to a Misbehaving Student

Let's say one of the students in your class keeps talking to other students while you're delivering a lecture. A very easy fix for this issue is to go over to the student and stand over their shoulder while you're teaching. Standing next to a student shuts down their misbehavior very quickly, as they're no longer hidden behind the rest of the class and are aware that you have noticed their misbehavior. When the student has stopped misbehaving, move away from them while making rounds throughout the class. When you're moving about in the class, it limits the students' ability to misbehave.

Prioritizing Relationships Over Retribution

Having a rapport with the students, establishing a relationship with them throughout the school year, and being personable effectively manage their class behavior. When every student feels like they can relate to you and feel like you're in their corner, they will not want to destroy their relationship with you. On the other hand, they will be obliged to facilitate and assist you as best as they can.

A healthy relationship with your students is a much better way to manage discipline in the class than retribution, blaming, labeling, and pointing fingers at them. While the former creates a collaborative and helpful environment in the class, the latter creates discord between you and your students while hurting their sentiments.

Rewarding Good Behavior

Positive feedback is always better than negative feedback. When you reward good behavior in your class, you incentivize every student to behave better. You're motivating them with rewards and praise rather than discouraging them with punishments and retribution.

Establishing Clear Rules and Being Consistent with Them

If you have been consistent with your rules throughout the year, whenever someone breaks a rule, they'll understand that you're just following procedure when you discipline them. They'll respect the process and accept their disciplining rather than rebel or lash out. This is because you've been fair and consistent in your behavior with the class and established clear rules for everyone to follow.

Identifying the Real Cause

Negative behavior is not the real issue in most cases. It's a symptom. If a student shows a lack of interest in the program, it might be because they face troubles that aren't as apparent. Perhaps they have a learning disability such as dyslexia or ADHD that hasn't been diagnosed yet. Maybe they're being so angry and disruptive in class because they're being victimized outside or even within the school. If they're constantly frustrated in the class, it's not because they're being difficult on purpose; there might be a legitimate cause such as physical impairment or a learning disability at play here.

The more experienced teachers, who have gone through several batches of students over the years, will be better equipped to notice symptoms of learning disabilities, abuse, or other problems in their students. For newer teachers, you should not hesitate to reach out with your concerns to experienced members of your school or the parents.

Suppose a student has undiagnosed ADHD and they're exhibiting the warning signs in the class. If you manage to help them in some way, whether by taking your concerns to their parents or making sure they get diagnosed, you will alter the course of their lives. Now they can get the help they need through therapy and medication and resume their studies without being frustrated. If you successfully identify the real cause of their misbehavior, you will save the student from the lifelong trouble that awaits them.

Helping Challenging Students

The teacher has to be impartial. Every student needs their help, especially those struggling or proving to be very challenging in the classroom. They might even need more help than regular students.

Troubling behavior often points to some underlying issue that needs to be addressed. It can also be a cry for help on the student's part. The age range of five to ten is very young, and it's difficult for students in that age range to vocalize their issues. To get attention, they try to misbehave or create disturbances.

To help them, you must look beyond their troubling behavior and deal with them professionally, calmly, and decisively. You can start by conducting a private question-and-answer session with those students. Chat with them and get to know them. Informally talk to them as you assess if some trouble is bothering them or if there are any issues you need to be aware of.

Make it known to the student that you are a safe person to come to. If you've already gained their trust in the classroom, perhaps they will confide in you about the trouble they're having. If not, you can ask them questions that reveal the nature of their problems.

Gather additional information about the student from other teachers and parents to find out how they learn and what they respond to the most. This will help you connect with them and create an easier learning environment for them.

If you talk to them after class in a non-confrontational way, it will dissolve the impression that you're just their teacher. It will help them look at you from a different perspective. You can be their helper or a friend. Ask them what their favorite in-class activities are, favorite types of lessons, and which exercises help them remember the key lesson points the best. Be frank with them as you discuss what helps them focus in their daily life. Talk to them about what they love to do outside of school. Ask them how they interact with their family at home. Is there someone in their family who they work well with, perhaps an elder sibling or a particular parent?

Now, you have two options ahead of you. If you sense an underlying issue that the student is struggling with, you should do your best to address that issue. Since you're the teacher, you must convey your thoughts and concerns to the parents. Only they can take the child to a doctor.

If there's no underlying issue, you can take your insights from the chat you've had with the student and integrate them into the class. We have already discussed how to do so in the personalized learning chapter. Now observe the student over the next few days and see how they respond to the new teaching techniques. Are they performing better than before?

You should also offer to tutor them after class if they share with you that they're not able to grasp the concepts adequately. During those tutoring sessions, you can form a closer bond with them which will help minimize their challenging behavior in class.

If you have noticed some underlying issue with the student, you should be very careful and respectful about the whole matter. When you talk to their parents or guardians, your tone should be that of genuine concern and well-meaning. There shouldn't be any condescension in your tone as you discuss this matter with their parents.

After implementing these tips and tricks, you will notice a gradual change in your class. There will be fewer and fewer disciplinary issues, paving the way for a smoother learning experience for everyone.

Conclusion

"You don't just teach - you inspire!"

Classroom management combines different teaching and management techniques that ensure an optimal learning environment for the students and the elementary school teacher.

Throughout this book, my goal was to share my insights, tips, and methods regarding managing a classroom effectively and thoroughly. From setting up rules to arranging furniture in the classroom, there were multiple important facets of classroom management that I shared.

In the first chapter, I introduced the concept of classroom management, explained its benefits, and defined the roles of an elementary school teacher. We built upon that foundation in the second chapter, titled "Setting Up Rules and Expectations," where we deliberated over setting up classroom rules and expectations.

Classroom Organization is a critical part of classroom management. From seating arrangements to utilizing classroom walls, you discovered various ways to organize your classroom for optimum success.

We looked at techniques and habits for student motivation and focus in the fourth chapter. This included how to start the class each day, how to choose positive language over negative language, and great words to use every day.

Forming a relationship with your students is an important role of the teacher and factors directly in how well the classroom is managed. In the fifth chapter, we discussed that and much more.

Chapter six discussed the different types of learners in the classroom and the VARK model. In chapter seven, we looked at the benefits of interactive learning and how to encourage it. Then we explored how important it was to make teaching fun for everyone - both you and your students!

Adding movement in the classroom creatively serves as an excellent way to boost student focus. In the ninth chapter, we discussed different ways to add movement in the class and the benefits of adding movement.

Different students learn through different methods. One size doesn't fit all. The tenth chapter discussed a detailed analysis of personalized learning and its benefits. You discovered actionable strategies that can help you implement personalized learning in your class.

Celebrating the success of your students in class helps to motivate them. In the eleventh chapter, I shared ten practical ways you can celebrate student success in class and what benefits that lead to.

Parents are an integral part of a child's life. In the twelfth chapter, you found useful strategies to connect with parents to build powerful relationships that serve the students.

Teaching, as with all professions, takes practice to perfect. And so we took a look at the common mistakes that teachers make and how you can avoid them.

Finally, the last chapter in the book was about maintaining discipline in the class and helping challenging students in their studies. I shared how to set up rules, keep track of the students' discipline, what mistakes to avoid when disciplining, and tips on minimizing discipline issues in the class. We also looked at how you can assist challenging students in class and how their behavior can be a symptom of an underlying problem.

I truly hope that reading this book has greatly benefited you and helped you understand the fundamentals of classroom management at an elementary school level. You can quickly implement the lessons you learned in your classroom and notice the positive effects.

Before you go, I have a small request to make. I would really appreciate it if you could review this book and share your lessons learned. Doing so will help me a lot in getting this book out to other readers, educators, and teachers who can benefit from the material I have shared.

Thank you so much for reading! I wish you many years of fun and happiness, educating and inspiring our next generation. Being an elementary school teacher is one of the most important job in the world.

Enjoy the next book in this series for elementary school teachers.

Made in the USA
Coppell, TX
11 February 2023